STEPS TO
SCHOOLWIDE SUCCESS

STEPS TO SCHOOLWIDE SUCCESS

Systemic Practices for
Connecting Social-Emotional
and Academic Learning

Stacey A. Rutledge
Marisa Cannata
Stephanie L. Brown
Daniel G. Traeger

HARVARD EDUCATION PRESS
CAMBRIDGE, MASSACHUSETTS

Paperback ISBN 978-1-68253-459-5
Library Edition ISBN 978-1-68253-460-1

Library of Congress Cataloging-in-Publication data is on file.

Published by Harvard Education Press,
an imprint of the Harvard Education Publishing Group

Harvard Education Press
8 Story Street
Cambridge, MA 02138

Cover Design: Endpaper Studio
Cover Photo: SDI Productions / E+ via Getty Images

The typefaces in this book are Adobe Garamond Pro and Helvetica Neue.

To the students of Broward County,
who inspired our focus on personalization
and continue to remind us about the
power of listening to students

Contents

CHAPTER 1

PERSONALIZING ACADEMIC AND SOCIAL-EMOTIONAL LEARNING
A New Approach to High School Reform

Consider the typical day of American high school students. They arrive before dawn at a large building bustling with other students and adults. Throughout the day, they travel from class to class usually in fifty-minute increments, jumping from *Romeo and Juliet* to mitochondria to the Civil War to symphonic band to isosceles triangles to Spanish verb conjugation, to volleyball, each class led by a different adult and populated with different students. Students may find some classes exciting, engaging, and motivating. They may experience other classes as tedious and uninteresting. They navigate through teachers' lectures, seat work, pop quizzes, collaborative work, discussions, and many other quizzes and tests. Some experience the academics of high school as highly demanding; others are working just to get through. Often, they are reminded by adults that their choices have serious consequences for their college and career opportunities after graduation.

As they navigate the academic side of schooling, students are also participating in a vibrant social environment. They interact with friends and other students in class, in the hallways, during their extracurricular activities, and on social media. Some students are involved with multiple friend groups and activities, whereas others are more reserved. Some find the social environment energizing. Others find it more stressful. For most teens, though, the social aspects are why they come to school: to play sports, to be in the school band, or just to hang out by the bus ramp with their friends and classmates.[1] Student interactions with peers are important in their adolescent development as these interactions influence their postsecondary plans, their motivation in school, how they value school, and their behavior.[2] Through their peer networks and friendships at school, students learn important social skills that help them feel engaged there.[3]

Today's teens also face challenges not experienced by prior generations. High-stakes testing and the pressures of accountability cause anxiety among many students as they prepare for exit exams, annual state testing, and college entrance and Advanced Placement (AP) exams.[4] Ninety-five percent of teens are connected by online social networks, and while most teens engage with their peers constructively, some experience cyberbullying, addiction, and depression.[5] Studies suggest that adolescents have higher levels of stress, depression, and suicide than do previous generations, although the reasons are not entirely clear.[6] While some research points to social media, students also face anxiety because of school shootings, other violence, and an increased security presence. If high school has typically been understood as a time of change and angst-ridden self-development, today's teens attend school with new layers of academic and social pressure as well as concerns about serious random acts of violence by their peers.

Besides their interactions with one another throughout the school day, students also observe and may interact with many adults, including teachers, guidance counselors, school custodians, lunch room workers, coaches, and administrators. Some students engage directly, participating in class, approaching teachers' desks, saying hello to adults in the hallway or cafeteria, and establishing positive one-on-one relationships based on a shared interest or involvement in clubs or athletics. A few teens are particularly adept at getting teachers' attention, but do so for negative reasons. Others, however, may choose not to engage with adults, staying quiet, sometimes remote, participating enough to get by, but avoiding interactions. Some students find it easy to reach out to adults, while others may expect caring adults to reach out to them. Student interactions with adults can be constructive and rewarding or uncomfortable and even distressing.

The adults in high schools also have different levels of engagement, motivation, and stress. Like the students feeling the pressure to perform and succeed, the adults are juggling multiple demands. Teachers multitask as they organize for each of their classes, grade papers, prepare students for state assessments, address individual students' emotional needs, work with colleagues, and deal with student behavior. While managing the expectations of their job, they may find interactions with students easy and want to improve adolescent social skills, or they may find these objectives secondary to their academic focus. As they seek to motivate students to perform academically, teachers rely on several strategies, including positive feedback, encouragement, accountability, tough love, and public humiliation. Like the students, teachers have different styles, reasons for working in schools, interests, and dispositions. When at the top of their game, they focus not only on academics but also on getting to know their students and linking instruction with students' interests.[7]

Every school day, teens navigate this complex social and emotional environment. Obviously, learning occurs in a social context, and high school is no exception.[8] Yet adults in high schools—with their bias on academics—often ignore the importance of the adult-student relationship in education. Students benefit academically and socially when they have in their lives adults who interact with and support them. They also benefit when these adults work within their organization to personalize the learning experience for students. In this book, we present our story of a school reform that has as its explicit purpose bridging the academic and social-emotional routines and activities through personalization. We describe the design and implementation of Personalization for Academic and Social-Emotional Learning (PASL), a reform that, through its five critical components, strengthens and links these practices in schools. PASL is a systemic approach to high school reform with the aim of improving high school students' academic, social-emotional, and behavioral outcomes. With PASL, adults in schools intentionally attend to students' interests and needs by engaging in organizational routines and norms of practice that institutionalize personalization. By deliberately fostering caring and supportive relationships with their students, adults help the teens increase their sense of belonging at their school. This sense, in turn, leads to higher levels of self-efficacy and student success. (PASL is not to be confused with personalized learning, whereby through teachers or computer programs, students receive curricular and instructional materials customized to their individual strengths, interests, and academic levels.)[9]

PASL is based on the idea that students' academic and social-emotional experiences are interrelated. Substantial research shows that student social-emotional competencies both shape and are shaped by their academic outcomes in school.[10] For example, teacher reports of the social-emotional skills of early adolescents predicted the students' later math and reading achievement.[11] Academic success in the classroom can lead to greater social integration in the school and classroom, and this integration contributes to the student's social-emotional development.[12] Beyond the academic benefits, social-emotional learning helps students manage emotions and stress, form healthy relationships with peers and adults, make responsible and ethical decisions, effectively communicate with teachers, and increase commitment to school.[13]

The PASL reform is more than a set of practices. As a new approach to developing and scaling school improvement, the reform provides time for educators to plan and systematically implement the reform practices and continuous-improvement strategies to accelerate learning and change across schools. PASL has been developed, implemented, and scaled since 2010 in Broward County, Florida, the sixth-largest school district in the United States. As we will discuss, in our capacity as codevelopers of PASL with the Broward County Public Schools, we started developing the reform with just three high schools, phasing in more schools each year. By 2019, thirty-two high schools and ten middle schools were implementing PASL. We credit the growth of PASL to the resonance of personalization strategies in schools and to the structured process that aims to build capacity in and across schools.

PASL has had positive outcomes for students and adults. Our belief that PASL improves student outcomes is informed by two separate evaluations, both of which represent results from a cohort of schools' first year of conducting PASL. The first evaluation focused on very early PASL implementation, and found that schools that faithfully apply the model have higher attendance and fewer major disciplinary referrals.[14] A subsequent evaluation on the first year of PASL implementation in schools that joined the PASL network later found that ninth graders in PASL earned more credits and had fewer disciplinary referrals than did their matched peers not in PASL. While these results did not quite reach the threshold of statistical significance, they are practically important since ninth-grade credit accumulation is a critical early-warning indicator for high school graduation (Internal communication with RTI International). Our confidence in PASL's impact on students is also based on the strong buy-in from Broward County Public Schools educators and their continued efforts to involve more students in PASL. These educators' commitment to PASL grew as they saw improvements in student grades, attendance, and disciplinary referrals for students participating in the reform. At the school level, administrators pointed to these findings as evidence of their accomplishments and reasons for continued engagement with PASL. At the district level, central office leaders pointed to these findings when convincing new schools to join the PASL network.

Beyond considering the outcomes for students, educators who implement PASL describe it as "what good teachers do." They appreciate the reminder to be intentional in their interactions with students. They also say that PASL improves their relationships with other adults at their school, helping them feel more connected, and research has found that this sense of connection increases satisfaction and retention. These outcomes for students and educators are consistent with other research on personalization that we discuss throughout the book. [15]

Personalization is not a new idea in education.[16] It has been around for at least thirty years, with calls to personalize school environments to help students build a sense of belonging with their school.[17] Here, we build on these prior conceptions with a model that personalizes educational environments by harnessing beliefs, practices, and routines already present in schools to make them coherent and systemic. It is this new and innovative approach—through five components and continuous-improvement practices—that we describe throughout this book.

Schools see multiple benefits—academic and social—by focusing on making their schools more emotionally supportive. Teachers, school administrators, and other school staff in high schools work with students through a particularly vulnerable and formative time in teens' lives. But the daily demands and stresses of educators often get in the way of making important academic and social connections. In helping educators reinforce existing practices while making clearer connections between them, PASL leads to healthier and more responsive high schools.

While adolescents clearly thrive in situations where they are motivated, affirmed, and listened to, American high schools still face immense challenges in providing an environment where the majority of students feel engaged and connected. High schools are often rigid and bureaucratic places where teachers hurry through their academic content and are discouraged by students who are struggling or seem detached. To be sure, it is frustrating when students forget their homework, fail to put their names on assignments, text their friends in class, and disrupt classrooms with behavior like talking in class to friends and insubordination. Teachers face legitimate challenges from students as the adults work through their day. However, there are good reasons for teachers, administrators, and other adults to improve their interactions with students and to reflect on how to make their classrooms and schools more emotionally supportive. Through their relationships, students learn how to regulate emotions, engage in positive social interactions, and meet personal goals constructively. Not only do students need these social interactions for their social development, but the interactions also help address potential feelings of alienation.[18] They increase student engagement with classwork and with the school generally. And studies show that this engagement not only has payback for students, but also is good for the adults.[19]

The Birth of PASL

We did not pick PASL out of a book, and we did not learn about it from a professional-development provider. Instead, we identified and developed the approach through an organic, multistep process that has been almost ten years in the making. In 2010, we formed a partnership with Broward County Public Schools to understand why some urban high schools performed better than other high schools did in the same county.[20] With funding through a grant from the US Department of Education, we called our organization the National Center on Scaling Up Effective Schools (NCSU) and sought to identify and learn from effective high schools and adapt and scale their practices to other high schools in the same district. We believed that a one-size-fits-all approach across districts and schools was unrealistic and shortsighted. By focusing on exemplary schools within districts, we reasoned that the schools would share similar policy contexts, resources, and district administrative oversight that would make applying their successes to other schools easier.

As we began the reform process, we did not presume what would make the higher performing schools more effective. While we had our hypotheses about which elements within the larger structure of high schools might make a difference, we were open-minded about what would emerge from our study of schools in Broward County. In 2010, policy makers and reformers were at the height of the standards and assessment movement, so one bet would have been that it was the quality of instruction. Decades of policies and reform efforts suggested that instructional quality would be the difference. Federal and state policy makers had long been focused on the curricular and instructional approaches of teachers, with the logic that certain teachers excelled at improving student performance.

Complaints about the academic quality of high schools have existed for decades. Beginning in the 1970s, people began to argue that the problem lay with academic rigor and quality of teaching. With high school students receiving diplomas without demonstrating the appropriate clear knowledge and skills, there needed to be greater focus on classroom activities. To make sure that teachers were delivering the required academic content, and spurred by anxieties about keeping up with students in other countries, state reformers began implementing different kinds of standardized assessments, starting with minimum-competency exit exams and moving to, in the early 2000s, curricular standards and standardized assessments across English, mathematics, social studies and science.

As the testing culture grew, policy makers and reformers began adding elements that reinforced the academic push in the classroom. Between 2002 and 2015, with the federal policy No Child Left Behind, schools were expected to show that students were meeting adequate yearly progress across multiple subgroups of students. Different states, including Florida, put in policies grading schools A through F according to student performance on the state assessments. In 2010, incentivized by the federal Race to the Top policy, states began including a test measure of student growth into teacher evaluations, orienting teachers toward students' progress in their classroom. These efforts ratcheted up the academic focus in public high schools, with administrators and teachers feeling immense pressure to focus on academics so that their school would receive a good grade and other positive evaluations. Taken together, plenty of evidence suggested that the testing focus was shaping teachers' instructional decisions and that better teaching had the potential to improve student performance. One possibility was that differences between higher and lower performing schools would be found in the classroom.

Another bet would have been on the strong integration of organizational systems in schools. Successful high schools, the research showed, have strong systems of effective components rather than specific onetime programs or structures. Systems such as quality instruction, a culture of learning and professional behavior, and learning-centered leadership work together to build school capacity.[21] Top-down approaches, where districts mandate programs or practices that targeted one or two particular departments of a school such as guidance or English, saw low success rates. Instead, what made high schools stronger was an integration of school organizational routines and culture with academic press and rigor for all students; robust, professional learning with clear accountability systems for educators; strong administrators as well as teacher leaders; and personalized learning connections with strong outreach to the school community. These findings from the broader research suggested we needed to pay attention to how schools worked as broader systems, not only in terms of delivering instruction but also in terms of providing a place that supported both students and adults.

We began the project with an open eye to what would emerge from our findings, knowing that high schools have often faced intractable problems and that reform has been challenging. While high school outcomes generally have been improving—with more students graduating and students' readiness for college on the rise—there continue to be some deeply troubling outcomes. For example, 15 percent of students fail to receive a high school diploma, and inequities exist across different groups of students.[22] Beside the lack of connection felt by many high schoolers, students of color, students from low-income families, and English language learners in particular are much less likely to perform well and graduate than are other students. Our initial aim was to learn how to make high schools more engaged places for students as well as more equitable and accessible for all students. We could not anticipate, however, how much our inquiry would end up focusing on instruction, the overall school organization, or a completely different issue.

Broward County Public Schools is a particularly interesting place to take on this question of why some high schools, located in the same district and with similar demographics, perform better than others do. The district is the sixth-largest in the United States and home to thirty traditional high schools. A large, diverse district with students of different races, ethnicities, and economic backgrounds, Broward County Public Schools is located on the east coast of Florida. Fort Lauderdale is its largest city, but there are others, such as Pompano Beach, Sunrise, Hollywood, Parkland, and Pembroke Pines. With beaches on the Atlantic running up the east side of the state, the straight angles of development next to the Everglades on the west, and ribbons of highways running in between, the county is a place of gated communities and bungalows, gleaming glass high-rise apartments and low-rise public housing complexes. It can take an hour to drive from one corner of Broward County to another, through tolls and stoplights, through neighborhoods of palm trees and miles of strip malls. There is usually a warm gentle breeze crossing the Florida peninsula.

Like other urban districts, Broward County Public Schools is diverse. Sixty-two percent of students are classified as economically disadvantaged. About 79 percent are students of color, with approximately 40 percent Black and 33 percent Latinx. Some 11 percent are eligible for English language learner services. The graduation rate of 84 percent is slightly lower than the state and national averages. Broward County's high schools have experienced greater racial segregation than in the past, with student exposure to students of other races steadily declining during the 2000s.[23] Taken together, the schools in the Broward County district face many of the challenges confronting other large urban districts nationally.

We knew that seeking answers to our questions would be a complex task and would require expertise from Broward County Public Schools as well as the universities in the NCSU partnership, so we put together a large team of both quantitative and qualitative researchers, professional-development experts, and leaders from the school district. This team became a networked improvement community (NIC).[24] Three of us authors of this book are researchers—from Florida State University, Vanderbilt University, and York College of Pennsylvania—and one of us, a former high school principal in Broward County Public Schools, has also served as NCSU's district liaison since 2011. Over the years, we have been joined along the way by researchers from other universities; almost twenty graduate students; members of the Education Development Center (EDC) and the nonprofit research organization RTI International; a professional learning facilitator from 808 Education; and, most importantly, many Broward County Public Schools district and school administrators, teachers, counselors, behavior specialists, and students. All have helped in the effort to make high schools stronger and more responsive places for students and adults. We share our story here.

Investigating High Performing Schools

With these complex challenges in mind, we formed a partnership in 2010 with Broward County Public schools to investigate why some schools in urban areas performed better than others did. Members of our team identified four district high schools—two higher and two lower performing—to examine this issue.[25] Once the four schools were identified, we conducted three visits, each visit a week long, at these four high schools in the fall, winter, and spring of the 2010–2011 academic year.[26] At each school, we delved deeply into how the school worked. Over the three visits, we interviewed the principal, assistant principals, counselors, department heads, and coordinators for exceptional student education (ESE) and English language learners (ELLs). We interviewed tenth-grade science, mathematics, and English teachers. We conducted focus groups of students and other teachers. In addition to talking to these various people, we observed classrooms to understand the quality of instruction. These observations were particularly helpful for determining if the differences between the schools had to do with teachers and instruction. To this end, we used an instrument called the Classroom Assessment Scoring System for Secondary Classrooms, to assess the quality of instruction for eighteen teachers of English, mathematics, and science at each school.[27] Finally, during our last visit at each school, we shadowed six students for a full day and interviewed them afterward to understand their daily experience during academic classes, free periods, lunch times in the cafeteria, and electives. Together, these different approaches helped us to get a holistic picture of each school.

When we started to analyze our findings across different stakeholder groups and areas, it became clear that something other than differences in instructional quality was going on at the two sets of schools. With the two-decade-long focus on strengthening the instructional core, we were surprised to find that teachers' instructional practices were ranked similarly across the four schools. We found that all four schools had overall scores in the middle range of the Classroom Assessment scale, with no significant differences between the higher and lower performing schools. These results held true, even after we controlled for academic track, grade level, subject, and time of year of the observation.[28] Indeed, we found that the main differences in instructional quality lay within schools and between tracks.[29]

Yet, the two sets of schools did have important differences. We had built our data collection and analysis around the work of Ellen Goldring and colleagues on school effectiveness.[30] This research identified essential components of effective high schools: quality instruction, rigorous and aligned curriculum, a culture of learning and professional behavior, learning-centered leadership, and connections to external communities. We added others: the systemic use of data, systemic performance accountability, and personalized learning communities. We developed our data collection instruments and our coding plan around these eight components and the research supporting their importance.[31]

Using this model of school effectiveness, we saw that efforts to personalize the learning experience for students at the high performing schools took many forms, including curricular and instructional activities in the classroom, teachers' professional development, communication with parents and other members of the school community, and school culture. Adults at the two higher performing schools talked about the different ways they sought to pay attention the student experience at their schools. English and chemistry teachers said they tailored their lessons to students' interests. Assistant principals and counselors explained how they looped, or kept a sustained ongoing connection with, the same groups of students over four years to build relationships with each student during their time at the school. Counselors talked about monitoring students' progress and sharing student data with teachers and other stakeholders during meetings of professional learning communities. Administrators communicated the importance of building trust with all members of the school community. They described how they had lunches with students, learned their students' names, and tried to consistently apply rules and regulations so that no student felt unfairly treated. Students, for their part, said they recognized the efforts teachers made to connect with them, either in the classroom, when teachers tailored curriculum and instruction to their interests or followed up on grades, or in the hallways, when adults said hello or when teachers reached out with suggestions about extracurricular activities.

We began to see that these different activities not only served as organizational routines, such as in the case of looping, but that they also solidified a culture in which low, medium, and high performing students alike felt that they were cared for and listened to. Further, efforts to personalize also appeared across components, and effective schools had systems that linked these components.

Interestingly, we also found a number of these practices at the lower performing schools. For example, some teachers described accounting for students' interests as they planned their lessons, and some counselors looped with students over three years. Teachers still met in professional learning communities and with their departments. Adults at the lower performing schools still sought to build connections with the parents and the community. They were avid users of data. However, these activities were not as pervasive, interconnected, and systemic as they were at the higher performing schools. Data activities, for example, were conducted individually, with little sharing across stakeholders. While individuals or pockets of people engaged in activities that supported students, the activities were not working as a system across the school. Students waited months to see a counselor. Counselors spent the majority of their time organizing school testing. Teachers expressed frustration at inconsistent administrative policies and poor communication. Teachers and students alike complained about inconsistent student discipline, with referrals languishing in administrative offices for days and students perceiving that certain students were favored over others.

As the evidence began to mount across the different groups participating in the study, we began to recognize that the higher performing schools fostered adult-student connections through intentional organizational and systemic personalization. In these schools, the adults built connections and trust with students and other adults through the standard organizational features of the high schools. We observed this trust in classrooms as teachers sought to connect their curriculum and instruction with students. We also saw it embedded in other systems and routines at the school, including the students' transition to the ninth grade, the use of data as a tool for personalization, and a general culture of caring. Once we had gathered our evidence, we met as a research team to comprehensively review it. Confident in our findings, we named this organizational and systemic approach Personalization for Academic and Social-Emotional Learning, or PASL.[32]

A Structured Design Process

With the identification of PASL as what differentiated the higher and lower performing high schools in Broward County Public Schools, we turned to the next step in our work, the design of a reform initiative. We wanted to translate our research findings into a reform that could be implemented in other Broward County high schools. We convened researchers from our partner universities—Vanderbilt, Florida State University, and University of North Carolina at Chapel Hill—developers from the EDC, and stakeholders from the district over several day-long meetings to turn the research findings into something that could be implemented in other high schools in the district. Members from three high schools—our pilot schools—attended the meetings, as did representatives from the district and educators from other high schools.

Over several months, we engaged in a structured design process, turning PASL into a set of practices that could be shared.

This design and development process, which we discuss in more detail in chapter 2, involved first drawing from other research findings to corroborate our observations of the higher performing schools. Comparing our findings to prior research, we established that others had indeed had similar conclusions about effective practices and approaches. For example, the literature on adolescent development supports our observations in the higher performing schools. The studies show that schools are centers of social interactions and that adults and students interact around curriculum and instruction, social activities, and the rules on discipline and behavior.[33] These interactions help adolescent mature, promoting student self-efficacy, self-agency, and a sense of belonging as well as important social skills. We also found research evidence that supported interactive practices such as looping; articulation, or sequencing, of the curriculum between middle school and high school; and instructional attention to students' interests.[34]

We then distilled the findings into the definition of PASL as a systemic approach to high school reform that attended to students' academic, social-emotional, and behavioral outcomes. Finally, we challenged the team to come up with an implementable model. With our strong belief that implementation needed to reflect local context and circumstances, we decided to establish components of our model for people to adapt, rather than a scripted program for people to implement.[35]

The Components of PASL

We identified five systemic personalization practices in the high performing schools we observed (figure 1.1). Together, these five

FIGURE 1.1 The five components of Personalization for Academic and Social-Emotional Learning (PASL)

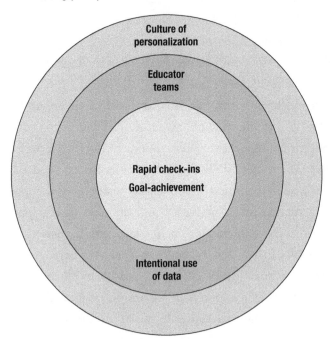

components of PASL provide a *system* of personalization that bridges the traditional academic focus of high schools, with approaches aimed at building relationships and helping students set goals, track their own academic progress, and feel connected to their school. For online tools related to the PASL components, please see https://my.vanderbilt.edu/pasltoolkit.

Rapid Check-Ins

Teachers at each school conduct routine *rapid check-ins* with approximately twenty students. By regularly checking in briefly with students, adults show that they are interested in, and care for, the students. These practices increase students' social-emotional competencies, which in turn improve their academic and behavioral outcomes.[36] Through these check-ins, teachers not only build relationships but also make sure students get the support they need so they do not fall through the cracks. The adults keep logs of their check-ins, making sure that over a set period, such as two weeks, they have had a conversation with these students. Conversations range from short discussions about last night's basketball game to more in-depth questions on a student's attendance. In the same way that teachers are accountable for their upcoming instructional approaches through lesson plans, PASL teachers are accountable for keeping track of their rapid check-ins with students. If the teacher decides that a student needs extra support, they identify the student to the guidance counselor or assistant principal for additional services.

Goal-Achievement Activities

PASL teachers also engage in *goal-achievement activities* with their students. Goal-achievement skills improve performance through better self-regulation of behavior, persistence, and other metacognitive skills.[37] Teachers plan customized activities that can be as short as three distinct lessons or as extensive as year-long activities. In goal-achievement activities, students set short- and long-term goals. As the teens document their goals on paper or through the support of technology, teachers learn about their students' individual interests. Teachers also return to these goals throughout the year and use them to help students have more responsibility over their learning. Students develop increased ownership of elements such as deadlines, time management, grades, and personal development. Through these goal-oriented activities, students work on and share their goals with their teacher, helping the teacher get to know their interests and challenges. In turn, teachers can use their more comprehensive view of each student when collaborating with other teachers and in their own classrooms.

Intentional Use of Data

In their rapid check-ins and goal setting, teachers *intentionally use data*, such as students' grades and attendance, to further identify students who need additional resources.[38] By examining student data, teachers probe deeper into root causes of students' challenges. Teachers may conduct quarterly data chats with students to return to student goals and monitor students' progress. Administrators and counselors also use data to inform their support for students. Using data purposefully, adults build better information about students, bridging the classroom and the school and thereby sharing with other adults their knowledge about a student and their progress through school.

Educator Teams

Administrators, teachers, and counselors convene regularly in *educator teams* to discuss students' academic and social-emotional progress. In these teams, adults collaborate on particular students' situations and determine appropriate interventions. They may also discuss or plan PASL activities. In some schools, these meetings are integrated into professional learning communities meetings, while in other schools, teams prefer to meet before or after school. Educator teams convene to discuss students' needs, in an effort to provide greater adult collaboration around those needs.[39] The members draw on information gained through rapid check-ins and goal-achievement activities as well as other kinds of evidence to share their observations and concerns.

Culture of Personalization

Finally, high performing schools promote a *culture of personalization*. Such a culture permeates these schools as adults connect with and learn about students through rapid check-ins and goal-achievement activities. This personalization culture is also built when teachers intentionally use data and meet in teams to discuss how to support students.

Attitudes and practices beyond the other four components of PASL can also instill a culture of personalization. For example, administrators and teachers can support students' perspectives and needs with action. Adults can help students find extracurricular activities that match their interests, can develop mentoring programs, and can encourage a culture where students feel that their individual needs are being met. Adults can also expect that students and adults speak with each other and otherwise interact. A culture of personalization is supported by research that shows the importance of school vision, mission, and culture around shared values and beliefs for a positive impact on student learning.[40]

Continuous Improvement Through Plan-Do-Study-Act

In designing PASL around these five components, we acknowledged that each school had its own dynamics and combination of stakeholders, culture, and policies.[41] Each participating school agreed to implement the five components of PASL and to adapt each component to its own situation. All the schools have their own unique version of PASL, building on prior programs and practices, and their own mission and vision, in an effort to meet the needs of both students and adults.

While we embraced the idea that each school had to adapt PASL in the way that best suited its culture, staff, student body, and community, we did require that participating schools engage in our process of continuous improvement to implement and adapt PASL. Every three months, the schools conducted quarterly cycle testing. We used the continuous-improvement approach called plan-do-study-act (PDSA). The PDSA approach works in the following way: implementers identify areas of improvement, test out a new approach, study the results, and act on their results. Each site is encouraged to start small, piloting PASL first with a small group of students, and then, over time and building on each cycle, adapting and improving on PASL at their school. In this way, PASL becomes a living reform, not something to be implemented and then completed, but rather something that is introduced, scaled, and adapted with different students and teachers over time. [42]

With studies showing that scaling is much more likely to be successful if schools build on their already-established programs and practices, we have found that PDSA allows implementers to measure improvement, modify current approaches, and iterate on new designs.[43] Our continuous-improvement model through PDSA was a major engine for the spread of PASL as well. At our quarterly meetings, school teams shared the findings of their cycles and their improved student outcome data. As schools reported fewer disciplinary referrals, stronger attendance, and fewer students on the D/F reports, for example, district and school administrators became convinced of the value of the reform. Teachers saw successes from their peers and asked to participate. As a reform codesigned by district and school participants, PASL represents an exciting new approach to high school improvement.

Implementing and Scaling PASL

Three schools—Blanche Ely High School, Charles W. Flanagan High School, and Piper High School—launched PASL in 2014. They designed their implementations in different ways, responding to their schools' existing practices and particular needs. The next year, five additional schools joined with their own introduction of PASL. Since 2016, twenty-two more schools have begun PASL, with all thirty traditional high schools, ten middle schools, and one alternative school of Broward County Public Schools now implementing the reform. Throughout this book, we will discuss these schools as they practiced PASL, describing the choices they made. We focus, in particular, on the first eight schools and their experiences, but we bring in examples from the other schools as well. We also discuss the schools' experience with the process of improvement.

In telling the stories of these schools, we aim to show the progress made and the setbacks encountered. No school had a straightforward trajectory of improvement. There were twists and bumps along the way, even with a committed and talented group of educators. We share these stories with the recognition that a school's story is never complete, but continues to evolve over time. We should note here that we use the real names of schools and most adult participants; however, we do not use the real names of students.[44]

Gaining Acceptance of PASL

Scaling PASL into thirty-one high schools and ten middle schools in Broward County Public Schools has taken five years. The district has embraced PASL as a central strategy to motivate students and school staff and consequently to improve student outcomes. In 2019, the reform became the district's official social-emotional initiative. People believe in its core mission to improve adult-student relationships in schools. It resonates with district and school leaders, teachers, counselors, and other school staff as they seek to address students' academic and social-emotional needs. We often hear from teachers that PASL is "what most teachers do naturally but it's making sure we do it with intention" and is "common sense for good teachers." The adults we have interviewed recognize that that they need to show students they care. As one teacher explained, "PASL is making the personal connection so that [students] can come to you and they know that you care." A principal noted that PASL helps teachers go beyond academics: "Before, they could not get past students' academic difficulties, and now they see the difficulties not as an attack on them personally, but as a sign that the kid may need help with something."

We attribute the scaling of PASL to two main factors. First, the idea of personalization resonates with adults in schools. Administrators, teachers, and other school staff recognize that reaching out to students is supported through clear practices and routines. They appreciate having a formal structure for this important interaction. With the fundamental concepts of PASL consistent with their ideas of how to interact with students, they wholly embraced PASL.

Second, the continuous-improvement approach, in which school teams meet quarterly to engage in PDSA, has proved to be a powerful way for schools to advance their implementation of the reform. Each school has developed its own PASL approach, in which they build on their own data collection and implementation. As discussed earlier, as administrators and teachers saw fewer student referrals in PASL classrooms and better student attendance and academic performance, they shared these successes with their colleagues and saw these colleagues buy into the reform. Through the continuous-improvement process, therefore, educators built local evidence that PASL had positive outcomes for students.

Other factors also contributed to school acceptance. Students participating in PASL programs reported greater connections with their teachers. Teachers participating in active PASL programs described stronger connections both with students and with colleagues. These connections with students and colleagues reminded teachers of their intrinsic motivation for entering teaching. Students appreciated the regular check-ins and acknowledged that there were adults who looked out for them in their large high schools. The teens described their engagement when they participated in the formal and informal activities related to their school's personalization efforts, including the regular tracking of activities, grades, and peer mentoring programs.

When the results of PASL were shared in the quarterly meetings, district administrators heard about school successes and put their support around the reform, encouraging other schools to join in and "start small" in their initial implementation. Teachers implementing the reforms, when kept involved in the process, also experienced the success of PASL and felt motivated to continue implementation. No matter how each participating school conducts its own journey with PASL, when the reform is implemented with integrity, the schools have been strongly committed to the implementation.

Overview of the Book

We began this chapter discussing the experience of teenagers in high school, navigating the complexity of adolescence, academic pressure, and social demands, in impersonal high schools. We recognize that high schools can be large places where daily stresses impede the kinds of genuine connections that can help students succeed. In the chapters that follow, we show how PASL emerged as a solution to this problem, and we examine in greater depth each of its components.

Chapter 2 describes the continuous-improvement approach we used in the development and implementation of PASL. An opening vignette shows how a practice called Cross-Talk emerged out of one school's continuous-improvement efforts and was gradually adapted and incorporated into other schools' repertoire of PASL practices. The chapter illustrates how a networked approach to improvement—such as the PASL network—allows a good idea to move from a hunch to a tested practice implemented at scale, and we highlight both the challenges and the opportunities involved in continuous improvement.

Chapters 3 through 7 describe the details of the five components of PASL: rapid check-ins, goal setting and achievement, the intentional use of data, educator teams, and the culture of personalization. Each chapter focuses on one component and opens with a vignette showing how that component is enacted in a particular school. The chapter then discusses the research base that validates that component. Educators and students explain how the element contributes to students' social-emotional and academic success, and additional vignettes illustrate how the same component was adapted or modified in other schools. Each chapter concludes by identifying the essential features of the component across its various forms.

In chapter 8, we reflect on PASL overall, placing it in the context of the evolution of the American high school and the pendulum swing of reform efforts over the past century. We explain why PASL has succeeded where past high school reforms have failed.

For readers, this book provides insight into a reform aimed at improving academic, social-emotional, and behavioral outcomes for students. It also describes an improvement approach that is gaining traction in the reform community for its power to enable stakeholders to adapt reforms to local contexts. Indeed, the story of PASL provides evidence for the ability of continuous improvement to build and grow effective reforms. Through stories and research; the voices of administrators, teachers, and students; and peer-reviewed studies, we present the case for attending to deliberate and systemic personalization.

CHAPTER 2

USING EVIDENCE TO IMPROVE PASL

Continuous Improvement in a Networked Community

Blanche Ely High School (Ely), located in the northeast section of Broward County, is named after a former principal and a civil rights activist. The school is deeply connected to this history. While it now houses a magnet program in health sciences and nursing and draws students from all over the county, it continues to play a central role in the neighborhood. Many of its teachers and students are the second or third generation in their family to attend the school. Demographically, the school is 82 percent Black, 12 percent Latinx, and 4 percent White, with an overall enrollment of just over two thousand students and an economically disadvantaged rate of 76 percent. The school's principal, Karlton Johnson, says his vision is to "make students meet their maximum potential." This vision aligns with the school's mission, "Destination Excellence," which highlights its academics while also supporting its championship football, basketball, and band programs. PASL also strongly fits into this vision. Johnson says,

"It's not just the grades itself. It's the social-emotional learning. It's the mental aspect of the child." The school has faced numerous challenges, including high teacher turnover and low student test scores. Still, it has a strong internal identity as a school rooted in the local community.

The PASL team at Ely participated in the multiyear design and development of the five PASL components. Ely, Charles W. Flanagan High School, and Piper High School together codeveloped the PASL reform and piloted specific practices in their schools. The Ely intern principal, Cherie Hodgson-Toeller, led the school's PASL team. The story that follows illustrates how one promising innovation—Cross-Talk—took root and spread through this process.

Early in the development process, the PASL teams from all three schools would meet monthly as a whole network to share evidence about the practices they had been piloting and what they had accomplished in their schools. These meetings were a time to share learning, refine practices, and discuss their results. At one such meeting, Hodgson-Toeller presented evidence of a culture shift at the school. She showed what her school had accomplished so far that year. Although she first focused on the PASL activities with students, Hodgson-Toeller became more animated about a process she called Cross-Talk, a practice within the educator-team component of PASL. A typical Cross-Talk occurred during regularly scheduled faculty meetings when an administrator handed out the current list of students who were failing at least one course. Because of state accountability requirements, teachers felt pressure from both the state and the district to reduce the number of students who were failing courses so that the students could stay on track to graduate. During the Cross-Talk, teachers identified one student they knew on the list and paired up with another teacher who also taught that student.

Usually, a teacher only knows the student's grade in the teacher's own course. Through the Cross-Talk process, teachers heard about how students were performing in other classes. For example, Justine may be on the list because she is failing Mrs. Tate's math class but is getting a B in Mr. Lopez's chemistry class.[1] When Mrs. Tate and Mr. Lopez meet in a Cross-Talk, they discuss their experiences working with Justine. By learning how Mr. Lopez engages with Justine, Mrs. Tate may stitch together a broader portrait of Justine than as a student who is failing her class. Cross-Talks thus create powerful opportunities for teachers to learn about students in a different context.

After describing the Cross-Talk process to the district PASL team, Hodgson-Toeller talked about the teachers' responses. It was "quite the aha moment for a lot of them," she said. While noting that not all teachers were on board yet, she said that Cross-Talk changed how teachers approached student failure. The practice facilitated greater collaboration among teachers about student needs. Teacher buy-in, always a challenge when implementing new initiatives, was improving. Hodgson-Toeller pointed to increasing teacher engagement across Cross-Talk sessions—an increase indicated by the depth of teacher responses on the form she had asked them to complete. Teachers approached the first Cross-Talk as a compliance activity, completing the requested form briefly, if at all. By the second Cross-Talk, they demonstrated substantive engagement, documenting several strategies used to engage the student in question. Hodgson-Toeller interpreted this evidence as suggesting that teachers saw value in the process and were thus willing to engage more deeply. She also provided evidence of PASL's impact on students. Through its Cross-Talks and other PASL practices, Ely had seen a notable decline in students failing at least one course. But to Hodgson-Toeller, the real impact was on school culture. She closed her presentation by noting, "We are looking at this as a cultural shift."

After Hodgson-Toeller's presentation, the other pilot schools, Flanagan and Piper, noted that they also struggled with building teacher acceptance beyond the few teachers on their team. Perhaps, the members wondered, Cross-Talk would work at their schools. Later that day, as team members prepared for the next phase of work in their schools, the Flanagan and Piper team members began developing plans for implementing a version of Cross-Talk in their schools. As PASL has spread to more schools, finding a way for teachers to discuss a potentially at-risk student with other teachers who teach the student remains a core practice.

Scaling Innovation Through Continuous Improvement

How Cross-Talk became a central PASL practice is an example of using evidence for continuous improvement.[2] More than a story about just one high school, it describes how a networked approach to improvement allows a good idea to move from a mere hunch to a tested practice implemented at scale. This is a chronic problem in education—how to scale up promising innovations. The education system lacks neither innovation nor research about innovation. Despite criticism that high schools have not changed in a century, educators are innovating all the time. In their teacher preparation and induction into teaching, teachers are socialized to see learning as part of teaching.[3] That is, the work of teaching also involves assessing what students have learned, adjusting one's teaching practice and trying something new when students have not yet mastered the content, and then assessing students again. Individual teachers are thus innovating, testing, and adjusting and learning from evidence all the time. What is lacking for widespread educational improvement is an infrastructure that allows that learning to expand to more educators.[4] How do we use evidence in one context to more broadly improve educational practice?

Bringing practices developed in one school or classroom to another can be difficult. Research on past efforts to scale up effective programs and practices has documented the challenges of building teacher buy-in, aligning with the organizational context, and developing capacity among educators at various schools and district central offices.[5] The results of these efforts at large-scale improvement have been disappointing, leading to calls to fundamentally change our approach to educational improvement at scale. What is needed, these scholars argue, is fewer efforts to exactly replicate proven programs and more opportunities for educators to use evidence to collectively learn about and improve practice.[6]

Continuous-improvement research and networked improvement communities represent one model for how to bring educators and researchers together around a shared problem of practice.[7] Continuous-improvement research moves beyond translating research into language that is accessible to practitioners, but aims toward building two-way communication bridges so that both educators and researchers learn from each other.[8] Further, this research keeps the focus on student outcomes, rather than on replicating proven programs exactly. We know that educators adapt programs as they implement them and that they need to adapt to make the programs work in their situations.[9] Continuous-improvement processes shift the attention from whether adaptation is happening to how to support productive adaptation.[10] That is, how do we help educators take a program or practice with known good results in one set of circumstances and integrate the core elements into their own practices? This type of adaptive integration requires building collective knowledge about how practices lead to educational outcomes.[11]

Networked Improvement Communities

Networked improvement communities (NICs) have emerged as a mechanism to support educators in building and mobilizing collective knowledge around complex problems and potential solutions.[12] These communities are most closely associated with improvement science and have been emphasized by the Carnegie Foundation for the Advancement of Teaching.[13] The idea behind NICs originated in the business field from a collaborative-software structure that focuses on enhancing the ability to improve. That is, the focus is not just on improving a basic function that supports the customer, but is on working across organizations so that any organization can improve its functions quicker.[14] When structured as a NIC, school teams learn not only from their own experiences but also from the experiences of other schools. As they are all focused on a shared problem of practice, the members of NICs can systematically pool individual insights into collective knowledge.[15]

A core strength of NICs is the presence of multiple partners, who each provide a different form of expertise.[16] The complexity of educational problems, explains Anthony Bryk, president of Carnegie Foundation for the Advancement of Teaching, and his colleagues, requires bringing together diverse forms of expertise "in ways that enhance the efficacy of individual efforts, align those efforts and increase the likelihood that a collection of such actions might accumulate towards efficacious solutions."[17] NICs have power not only because of the people they bring together, but also because of their shared definition of the problem and systematic collection of evidence about the solutions. The sustained engagement of multiple stakeholders with ongoing discussions of evidence leads to organizational learning and effective adaptation.[18] This collective building of knowledge continues after the initial innovation is developed, as partners test the practices and share their learning with the broader partnership.

NICs are both design communities and learning communities that engage in research and development while also arranging human resources and knowledge-based tools to organize improvement work.[19] The communities form around goals shared by multiple organizations and use a variety of tools, such as common metrics, program improvement maps, and a shared theory of improvement. Furthermore, the plan-do-study-act (PDSA) cycle, or similar structured inquiry protocol, helps provide a common system of measurement to build shared knowledge.[20]

The effort by the Carnegie Foundation for the Advancement of Teaching to improve graduation rates in community colleges is perhaps the best example of a NIC in education.[21] To reduce the high failure rates in developmental mathematics courses, the foundation designed a program that included a new mathematics curriculum and other resources. Faculty who are following the foundation's program across several community colleges test and refine the instructional resources using a PDSA inquiry protocol. As individual faculty members test their own practices, their work can contribute to the broader knowledge base about this program through NIC meetings. The network structure allows knowledge gained by any individual to be accessed by others. This NIC for a community college demonstrates the potential for these networks to support educational improvement at scale. The foundation's efforts at NICs have increased course completion rates in developmental mathematics and nearly tripled the number of students served.[22]

As a strategy to achieve scale, NICs have several advantages. While some reformers equate scale as simply the number of schools implementing a given practice, our definition of scale emphasizes attaining deep and consequential change in schools.[23] Success at scale is not just about implementing a particular practice in a large number of classrooms. For us, success means a deep change in practice—and the beliefs and ideas that serve as the foundation of practice—in a way that is owned and made sustainable by local educators.

A core feature of NICs is the development of a shared theory of improvement that unpacks the focal problem of practice and applies it to the environment that educators are trying to improve.[24] This shared theory of improvement minimizes the tendency of school reform efforts to effect only superficial changes in classroom practices.[25] And locally directed improvement efforts are enhanced through a NIC, which allows educators to adapt practices to their own situations and to test the impact of these practices through a PDSA cycle.[26]

Innovation and adaptation are not new in school reform efforts, yet continuous-improvement approaches to scale can bring discipline to the adaptation process as school teams share evidence of what they have accomplished with others focused on the same problem.[27] This disciplined approach to improvement ensures that educators are making evidence-based decisions about which practices to implement and how to implement them, as multiple forms of evidence are examined to test and refine the practices in their context. By involving educators in cocreating practices for their environment, this approach can also foster a sense of ownership.[28] Further, a NIC provides the central infrastructure to facilitate learning across schools so that evidence gathered at one school can help inform the work at all schools.[29]

The PASL Network

Our partnership with Broward County Public Schools used two key structures to operate as a NIC: district and school PASL teams. As described in chapter 1, the partnership began in 2010 by intensively studying two higher performing and two lower performing high schools. The findings from that year-long investigation, which provided the basis for PASL, were summarized in a report for our lead district partner. At this point, two important decisions were made. First, the district identified three high schools that would serve as the pilot schools. Second, we established the district PASL team with a charge to develop a strategy for scaling PASL to more high schools. The district PASL team was composed of about eighteen members, drawn from a variety of backgrounds (figure 2.1):

- *Pilot school members:* Six members of the district PASL team were drawn from the three pilot schools (two from each school). There were three teachers, one guidance counselor, one media specialist, and one assistant principal.
- *At-large members:* Nine members of the team were drawn from nonpilot high schools or district offices and were considered at-large members of the team. They constituted three district administrators (one researcher and two curriculum specialists), five teachers, and one assistant principal.
- *Researchers:* Two members of the research team sat on the district PASL team. Both these researchers took part in the initial research on higher performing and lower performing schools in the district that identified PASL as the design focus.
- *District liaison:* This member of the district PASL team served as a conduit of information and communication with the district leadership and pilot schools, in addition to contributing as a member of the team.
- *Program developers:* Facilitating the work of the district PASL team were four program developers from the Education Development Center (EDC). The facilitators played a key role in coordinating the district team's activities, developing camaraderie and other good relationships among the team members and shaping team input into a coherent strategy.

FIGURE 2.1 Composition of district PASL team

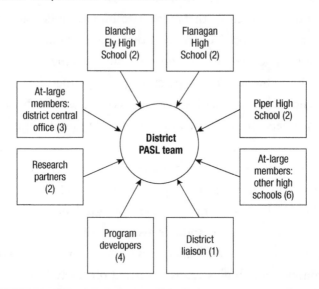

Source: Modified from Marisa Cannata, Lora Cohen-Vogel, and Michael Sorum, "Partnering for Improvement: Communities of Practice and the Role in Scale Up," *Peabody Journal of Education* 92, no. 5 (2017): 669–588, available at www.tandfonline.com/doi/full/10.1080/0161 956X.2017.1368633.

This composition of the district PASL team was intentional to ensure a diversity of expertise and perspectives that make NICs successful.[30] We included central office members because they could ensure continuity with other district priorities and processes, could advise on the availability of adequate district resources, and could stay on top of any potential districtwide constraints (e.g., new curriculum, teacher evaluation). Because the pilot schools would be the first sites of implementation, the district PASL team included two representatives from each of these three schools. Their inclusion allowed the district team to develop the PASL strategy while also attending to school-level adaptation. Representatives from other at-large high schools were also selected to represent the views of other Broward County schools where the innovation might eventually be scaled. The two researchers provided expertise on the PASL findings and other high-leverage practices identified in broader research. Finally, a district liaison served as a communication channel between the district and school personnel and the external partners and helped orchestrate the logistics of all the meetings.

Except for the researchers and program developers, the district team members were selected by district senior leadership, with input from the district liaison. The district leaders were encouraged to consider the following criteria when selecting team members:

- three or more years of demonstrated experience in leading change in schools or implementing programs related to PASL
- a reputation among colleagues as a well-respected opinion leader in the school or district
- interest in, and commitment to, serving on the district PASL team
- willingness to listen while exploring new ways of thinking about change
- effective verbal and written communication and presentation skills
- the ability to experiment and tolerate ambiguity
- the ability to examine and use data as a part of decision-making
- willingness to commit the time necessary to participate in team meetings and activities

The district PASL team's purpose was to build district capacity for identifying problems, designing and testing solutions, and supporting improvement at scale.[31] We referred to the district PASL team as the "owner" of the joint work for the district and the "keeper of the vision." In reality, while we sought to always involve district leadership in decisions about the district team's agenda and activities, research practice partnerships are always faced with dilemmas of hierarchy and establishing equality among partners when making decisions.[32]

The district PASL team had four primary responsibilities:

1. Study and interpret the research findings to determine the implications for innovation designs.
2. Use rapid prototyping to develop an innovation to be implemented, tested, and adapted in three high schools.
3. Develop a process for monitoring this implementation, and regularly collect data on progress.
4. Use the data to refine the innovation designs, revise the implementation process, and strategically plan for internal (in the three pilot schools) and external scaling (in other district schools).

These responsibilities were taken on through a series of meetings in which the district PASL team met as a group, first by itself and then after a day-long meeting of all school PASL teams. Table 2.1 summarizes the various phases of the partnership activities the district and school teams conducted to design and implement PASL.

The Design Phase: Identifying a Broad Strategy

The district PASL team met five times, each meeting two days long, during the design phase. In these first meetings, the members took several steps to examine the research and to identify an overarching strategy. They examined the research conducted in the four case study schools that led to the focus on PASL. The team also gathered and analyzed other evidence about PASL in the pilot schools. The team members engaged in additional activities to understand student needs around PASL. And they brainstormed systemic approaches to building student-teacher rela-

TABLE 2.1 Timeline of district and school PASL team activities

Phase	Period	Improvement community
Design	Fall 2012	District PASL team studied research findings and identified initial PASL strategy.
Development	Winter and spring 2013	District PASL team developed the strategy into an initial set of practices; school PASL teams formed in three pilot schools.
Initial implementation	2013–2014	District and school PASL teams jointly developed innovation, engaging in PDSA cycles of testing.
Full implementation	2014–2015	School PASL teams led full implementation of fully developed innovation in their school; continued engagement in PDSA cycles of testing; conducted quarterly network meetings of all PASL teams to share learning and plan for scaling in and out.
Scale-out	2015–2016 and beyond	District PASL team gradually assumes responsibility for facilitating network and supporting work in schools; between five and eight new schools join the network each subsequent year; school PASL teams continue to engage in PDSA and share learning in quarterly meetings.

Source: Modified from Marisa Cannata, Lora Cohen-Vogel, and Michael Sorum, "Partnering for Improvement: Communities of Practice and the Role in Scale Up," *Peabody Journal of Education* 92, no. 5 (2017): 669–588, available at www.tandfonline.com/doi/full/10.1080/0161 956X.2017.1368633.

Note: PASL, Personalization for Academic and Social Emotional Learning; PDSA, plan-do-study-act.

tionships and integrating academic and social-emotional learning. Through these activities, the district PASL team developed a core component of NICs: a shared understanding of the focal problem of practice and a shared theory of improvement about how various practices might improve that problem.[33]

Specifically, the initial research on the case study schools found that the key difference between the higher and lower performing high schools was an intentional and systemic focus on integrating students' academic, social, and behavioral experiences in schools. As we discuss on these pages, we call this integration PASL. The team members began by reviewing this finding in detail. They found that this effective integrative approach, or PASL, required several elements. For example, adults needed to model effective academic behaviors for students. Schools needed to provide students with opportunities to improve their capacity to recognize and manage emotions, solve problems, and establish positive and productive relationships with others. And the adults in the school should model behaviors and teach skills that foster social-emotional growth.

Each of the three pilot schools analyzed data about students' academic, behavioral, and social-emotional experiences. The data included scores on the state's standardized assessment, attendance records, behavioral referrals, and a survey about student engagement and sense of connection. The team's analysis of the data uncovered several common needs in the schools. First, although both students and adults thought that academics were satisfactory, achievement scores had decreased from ninth to tenth grade. Second, many students had excessive absences, and some students felt disengaged and lacked any connection to adults in the school. And finally, teachers needed strategies that connected academic learning and social-emotional learning. Brainstorming surfaced several ideas related to the explicit teaching of skills and behaviors for students to engage academically, socially, and emotionally in school. Goal achievement, with a large evidence base that it builds skills like self-regulation and persistence, was particularly important to the team, especially since members wanted to help students reach their college and career goals. The team agreed on the need for a tool kit of strategies and a curriculum for teaching these skills to students. The skills would be explicitly taught, perhaps in a homeroom, and reinforced in academic classes.

At the end of the design phase, the district's PASL strategy was defined as three broad themes to infuse PASL practices across the school and curriculum. The first theme focused on developing educator teams (including administrators, counselors, and teachers) assigned to follow a cohort of students over their high school career. These educators would mentor the students, receive information specific to their assigned students, and engage with each other through formally structured professional learning opportunities. The second theme was the explicit teaching and modeling of academic and social- emotional skills and behaviors. The third theme centered on the use of data to support PASL.

The district PASL team's focus on social-emotional skills is consistent with a growing national recognition that students need support in developing the behaviors, learning strategies, and mindsets necessary after high school.[34] Indeed, schools are tasked with not only preparing students academically, but also ensuring they become independent and involved citizens who, as Eva Oberle and coauthors explain, "are ready to responsibly navigate their own personal and professional pathways into early adulthood."[35] In Broward County Public Schools, this goal is known as being "college, career, and life ready." To achieve such a goal, students need support in developing social-emotional competencies that contribute to long-term outcomes such as greater educational and economic attainment, civic engagement, and mental health.[36]

The Development Phase: A Network of School-Based Teams

With these three themes of the PASL strategy identified, the district team turned to transforming them into specific practices. At this phase—development—each of the three pilot schools established a school PASL team. The purpose of these teams was to further develop, adapt, test, and implement the innovation in their school. Each school team had three to five members, in addition to an assistant principal who served as the coordinator of their respective school team and represented their school on the district PASL team. Of the three school PASL teams combined, ten members were teachers, three were assistant principals, and one was a counselor. The team members were appointed by their principal and were sometimes also recruited by district PASL team members in their school. The district PASL team members and principals were encouraged to select school team members for their either formal or informal leadership qualities, such as being highly respected among peers or a highly accomplished teacher.[37]

In the development phase, the school PASL teams met as an entire network for three meetings (each meeting was two days long) and two webinars. The goal of these meetings was to begin to develop the mindset critical for a NIC with a shared understanding of the focal problem, a shared theory of improvement, and a disciplined examination of evidence as the innovation practices were developed.[38] During the first two-day meeting, the school team studied the original PASL research and the district team's design process. In the second two-day meeting, the members reviewed evidence gathered from each of the pilot schools as the district team members shared the three PASL themes and school teams planned to obtain broader stakeholder input. They also broke into three working groups to work in depth on each of the three themes, or strategies. Within these working groups, they planned ways to further develop these strategies and discussed what they needed to investigate. The two webinars mostly provided updates to the whole network about the progress of each working group. At the final meeting of the year, each of the working groups shared its progress, and the school PASL teams began outlining how they might implement changes on a small scale the following school year.

At the end of the development phase, the five PASL components had begun to take shape through the three working groups. Rapid check-ins grew out of the first working group, as the members developed routines through which the educators could build mentoring relationships with students. The working group developed the idea of intentional points of contact, the first one being a rapid check-in, with support for more focused student-teacher interactions if the check-in suggested that the student needed additional attention.

The second component, goal setting and achievement, developed as the second working group focused on what social-emotional learning skills should be taught and how to teach them. The group initially explored using an existing curricular package that some schools in the district had implemented. This idea was consistent with the history of the district. "We don't build things," one district leader told us. "We buy things." The team members reviewed the materials and talked with individuals who had worked with this curriculum. They also organized focus groups at each of the initial three pilot schools to share the suggested curriculum and get feedback. In light of both the working group's review of the research on social-emotional development and the needs of PASL and district priorities, the skills in the suggested curriculum were organized around goal achievement. These skills included helping students set goals, develop an action plan, and then monitor progress toward their goals, as well as managing emotions, handling stress, and managing relationships.

The third PASL component—the intentional use of data— grew out of the third working group's focus on infusing data throughout most PASL activities. This group focused on what indicators to track and then outlined ways for educator teams to support students through the use of these indicators. The group selected five indicators of PASL's impact on students: course failure, grades in core subjects, attendance, behavioral referrals, and participation in extracurricular activities. The extracurricular activity indicator was adopted in recognition of two findings. First, the initial case study research found that Broward County Public Schools students often named leaders of their extracurricular activities as important mentors and as individuals in the school to whom they felt connected. Second, external research has suggested that participation in extracurricular activities is associated with increased achievement and reduced likelihood of dropping out.[39]

The fourth and fifth PASL components, educator teams and a culture of personalization, developed from the first working group. The group outlined the membership of those teams, how the members should work together, and how these teams would support the work of the educators. These ideas included time for educators to meet to discuss both student concerns and any necessary adjustments to PASL implementation. In fleshing out how the educator teams would work, this group highlighted the importance of attending to norms and culture for implementing the PASL reform, in addition to specific practices.

Initial Implementation Phase: Disciplined Inquiry

In the initial implementation phase, the NIC structure became more formal as school PASL teams began engaging in PDSA cycles of disciplined inquiry. The school teams were introduced to these cycles early in the initial implementation phase through formal training that occurred about every month in either face-to-face meetings or webinars.[40] Training around the inquiry cycles was supported by the researchers facilitating the pilot school PASL teams, all three of which were conducting the first two PDSA cycles around the same practice. Working as a NIC, all three school PASL teams aimed to learn about a teacher professional-development module that trained PASL teachers in rapid check-ins (i.e., they *planned* to test the professional-development module). The professional development occurred during an upcoming teacher planning day (i.e., the *do* part of PDSA). At the next meeting, when the school PASL teams brought in the data they had collected on the teacher development module, the school PASL team members collectively discussed what they had learned and what the implications should be for PASL (*study*).

For example, the data indicated that the time allotted for the module was appropriate and that the content was well received, despite concerns raised about how to monitor rapid check-ins and several suggestions on how to organize the handouts better for a new audience. With this evidence, the school PASL teams decided to make the small suggested changes to the handout and to focus next on the rapid check-in process itself (*act*). As these teams continued to test the same practice, they planned a test around a way to document rapid check-ins. The evidence was brought back to the following meeting to continue the PDSA cycles.

The introduction of the PDSA cycle to the network thus had some success in the initial implementation year. Indeed, all members saw value in the process, with some espousing real enthusiasm.[41] Yet engaging in the cycle was not without its challenges. Despite the members' appreciation, they also expressed frustration, saying that there was too much paperwork or that documenting all the data was too time-consuming. Most participants reported sufficient personal capacity to engage in PDSA through both the training provided to the network and prior exposure to continuous-improvement processes. Yet some people continued to be confused about the purpose of collecting and analyzing data beyond tracking a few key indicators to evaluate whether the broader goals of PASL had been met. The largest challenge was finding enough time for the systematic collection and analysis of process-level data that could help link specific practices to those broader outcomes.

Despite these challenges, people also believed that the PDSA cycle was a productive way to develop the PASL practices. At one point, a teacher referred to the cycle as "broccoli," suggesting that while some teachers and staff may not always like it, they recognized the cycle's value in a healthy improvement process. As the process moved to the full implementation phase, network meetings became less frequent, occurring quarterly rather than monthly, but the routines and norms that had been established the prior year persisted. Where the research team and program developers structured PDSA cycles for all schools around the same practice in the initial implementation phase, in the full implementation phase, each school decided on its cycle independently, with continued support and check-ins every two weeks.

Hearing the need for more time to engage in the PDSA cycle, the network meetings also included more time for school PASL teams to complete their data analysis. A typical network meeting began with an activity meant to build a sense of community among members and to refocus on the goals of PASL. Then, the school teams had some time to finish their systematic analysis of their own data and their reflection on the past cycle. In this way, the teams came to a common understanding of what was learned within each school. Next, a representative from each school team shared the results of their recently completed PDSA cycle, including which practice they had focused on, what evidence they had examined, what they had learned, and the implications of their learning for future PASL activities. This report was followed by a network-wide discussion of what was being learned across schools. Sometimes, we as researchers would also present evidence from our own data collection activities, such as interviews and observations. These activities made the learning in one school accessible to all the schools and included some explicit capacity-building for PASL team members around specific ideas. For example, the network looked at the role of school leadership in support of PASL, how to gain teachers' acceptance, and how to use data to support students. After lunch, the school teams planned their next cycle, and the network outlined the implications of their shared learning for the district PASL team meeting the next day.

The Development and Scale-Up of Cross-Talk

During the initial implementation of PASL, Hodgson-Toeller and the Ely PASL team began developing Cross-Talk. Near the end of the initial implementation phase, Ely had been part of the PASL network for about two years. During this time, they had uncovered the initial research findings on the district's need for an intentional PASL strategy in its high schools. They had also engaged with the district PASL team to develop a framework for that strategy, and had piloted the practice of rapid check-ins. Up to this point, the focus had been on adult-student interactions through these check-ins. Educator teams were one of the five components of PASL, but exactly how the adults in the school would collaborate to support students had been left unspecified. What's more, rapid check-in data indicated that the same students were usually requiring follow-up, further suggesting that the adults needed a way to discuss students in more depth among themselves.

Hodgson-Toeller and her team had an idea to have teachers discuss the students they shared. To try out this idea, Hodgson-Toeller recruited a small group of teachers, along with a counselor and an administrator, some of whom were also on the school's PASL team. Near the end of the initial implementation phase, Hodgson-Toeller brought these teachers together and had them discuss a list of students who were on what is called the "D/F report." This report listed the students who were currently earning a D or an F and who were thus at risk of failing in at least one class. She gave the teachers a few broad questions to guide their discussion: How is this student doing across all their classes? What strategies can we use to move this student off the D/F report? After this meeting, the participants completed a feedback form about their experience. The school PASL team analyzed this feedback and summarized it for the rest of the network. The key observation they shared was that PASL teachers found it powerful to discuss their different perspectives on the same student. The team also had suggestions for how to improve communication among various participants. After sharing this learning, Ely High School began planning for full implementation the following year. Cross-Talk made its first appearance as a PASL practice.

In the full implementation phase, Cross-Talk continued to be a focus of Ely's PDSA cycle. A schoolwide pairing of teachers for Cross-Talk was again received as a powerful way to gain a positive perspective on a struggling student. Yet, documentation of what happened because of Cross-Talk continued to be a concern. Hodgson-Toeller adapted how she asked teachers to report the strategies used to engage students on the D/F list. Rather than ask teachers to return a form, which was often lost, she began sending emails that teachers could reply to directly. Over time, Hodgson-Toeller and the Ely PASL team had evidence that Cross-Talk was beginning to change the culture of the school. When she shared her evidence on deepening engagement and greater teacher buy-in to PASL at the quarterly network meeting, the two other pilot schools were listening. That afternoon, as they planned the next PDSA cycle in their schools, they included a version of Cross-Talk. Figure 2.2 illustrates how PDSA helped scale Cross-Talk in the district. Early cycles focused on deepening and improving Cross-Talk within Ely High School. Then, once other schools saw evidence of increasing teacher buy-in and positive impact on students, they began adapting Cross-Talk on their campuses.

One educator who listened to the evidence Hodgson-Toeller presented was Derek Gordon. He joined the district PASL team at the start of the design phase, as a teacher representing an at-large high school. When the full implementation phase was nearing completion, Gordon was an assistant principal whose school was slated to be one of the first schools to begin the PASL scale-out.

FIGURE 2.2 A plan-do-study-act (PDSA) ramp for the development of Cross-Talks in PASL reforms

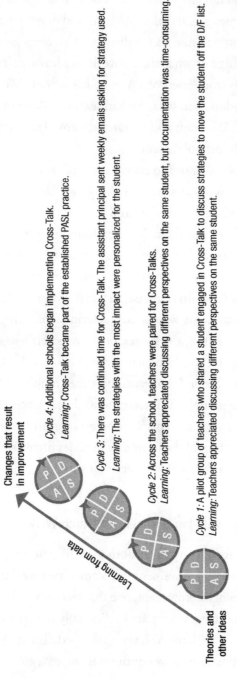

Changes that result
in improvement

Cycle 4: Additional schools began implementing Cross-Talk.
Learning: Cross-Talk became part of the established PASL practice.

Cycle 3: There was continued time for Cross-Talk. The assistant principal sent weekly emails asking for strategy used.
Learning: The strategies with the most impact were personalized for the student.

Cycle 2: Across the school, teachers were paired for Cross-Talks.
Learning: Teachers appreciated discussing different perspectives on the same student, but documentation was time-consuming.

Cycle 1: A pilot group of teachers who shared a student engaged in Cross-Talk to discuss strategies to move the student off the D/F list.
Learning: Teachers appreciated discussing different perspectives on the same student.

Learning from data

Theories and
other ideas

Source: Modified from Gerald J. Langley, Ronald D. Moen, Kevin M. Nolan, Thomas W. Nolan, Clifford L. Norman, and Lloyd P. Provost, *The Improvement Guide: A Practical Approach to Enhancing Organizational Performance,* 2nd ed. (New York: Wiley, 2009), 103.

That is, although his school was not one of the original pilot schools that engaged in the early testing and development of PASL practices, Gordon's role on the district PASL team gave him first-hand knowledge of what the network had learned. Tasked with leading the introduction of PASL to his school (Western High School), Gordon used what he had learned. Western formed its own school PASL team and rebranded Cross-Talk as the Wildcat Chat, after the school mascot.

The school continued to collect and analyze data on the implementation of Wildcat Chats, making two changes. First, after organizing Wildcat Chats around students on the D/F lists, as Ely High School had done, Western found that its own students on the D/F lists tended to have multiple low grades and required more extensive support than what could be achieved through a short Wildcat Chat. In response, the school began asking teachers to nominate students who were "teetering," meaning they were not necessarily failing any classes, but were nevertheless struggling academically and would benefit from the focused attention of a Wildcat Chat. Second, by examining the completed forms after the chats, the school PASL team noticed that teachers tended to rely on the same intervention strategies for all students. In response, the bottom of the form now includes fifteen strategies that may be relevant for particular situations.

Making Continuous-Improvement Research Work

The PASL reform consists of both a set of practices and an approach to school improvement. Educators interested in a new approach to school improvement, one that recognizes the limitations of how improvement efforts are traditionally structured, can learn a lot from the way that PASL was developed. The development of Cross-Talk illustrates how continuous-improvement approaches can address long-standing challenges in spreading school reform. First, having educators develop practices for their school builds local ownership. The Ely High School team began with a few teachers who believed in the vision of PASL. By testing the practices themselves, they could talk about the changes they were seeing in students when the practices were disseminated to more teachers. They also responded to feedback from teachers. The team held teachers accountable for the attempting the desired practices but also adjusted the accountability processes when the teachers indicated there was too much documentation. This bottom-up approach to school improvement also attends to the need for some accountability and system-wide infrastructure.[42]

Second, continuous improvement requires the use of multiple forms of evidence. In Broward County, as in many districts throughout the country, educators tend to focus on a few key student outcome indicators, such as test scores, attendance, disciplinary referrals, and grades. This focus makes sense in the context of high-stakes accountability in American high schools, where the focus is on ensuring that students are on track to graduate and be college and career ready. Yet, other forms of evidence can serve as valuable indicators of improvement. Attendance and test scores may tell you what you have achieved, but not which practices helped you get there.

The goal of continuous-improvement research and the PDSA cycle is to provide more fine-grained evidence that links the practices to the outcomes. For Cross-Talk, a core piece of evidence came from the implementation of the practice and improving how educators collaborated around student needs. Similarly, when Western High School turned Cross-Talk into its Wildcat Chats, it also collected evidence on the depth of teacher discussion in chats, as evidenced by the interventions selected. Across all the PDSA cycles conducted through the PASL network, a wide variety of evidence was collected. We also conducted interviews, focus groups, and observations that were fed back to school teams to improve both school- and district-level support processes. We surveyed students and teachers about their experience with implementation. One school PASL team created its own data system to track student interests and needs as identified through rapid check-ins. The data was eventually integrated into the districtwide data system.

Third, schools learned more as a result of working together as a network. The district PASL team initially involved three high schools, providing the opportunity for the collaboratively designed practices to be tested *at the same time in multiple settings*. Information about how the specific PASL practice worked in each setting established a knowledge infrastructure that all schools could rely on as they developed their own plans for implementing and disseminating the reform in their school.[43] Because the school teams were networked, they were not operating in a vacuum. The networking facilitated social learning across institutions and built up collective knowledge about PASL and its implementation.[44]

Fourth, developing educators' capacity and mindset for continuous improvement requires ongoing training and support. While most Broward County educators had experience with a general approach to continuous improvement and with analysis of student data, a systematic approach to continuous improvement requires a different type of data analysis than existing practice. It asks educators to specify, in advance, how they will know if any given innovation is an improvement. What form of evidence will they collect, often designing the indicator themselves, to monitor their progress? To build educator capacity, we created a workbook with suggested forms of evidence for different types of PDSA cycles, offered several formal learning opportunities (both face-to-face and online), and facilitated the first PDSA cycles while gradually shifting ownership of the reform to the school teams.[45]

This was not an easy process, as the early frustration with PDSA demonstrated.

Beyond training around the PDSA cycle, integrating continuous improvement requires that stakeholders have a shared view on a broad array of evidence for decision-making.[46] This cultural orientation toward evidence-based improvement requires two key shifts for educators. The first shift is from using data primarily for accountability to using it for learning and improvement. To make this shift, educators need to feel free to experiment without fear of being held accountable for any data collected. This change is not easy in an era of test-driven, high-stakes teacher evaluation and school accountability. Second, educators must recognize that improving individual practice is not the same as making improved practice systematic. The goal of continuous-improvement research is not just to support individual educators in learning about their practice, but is to develop systems that help groups of educators improve their practices. To this end, any learning by an individual educator should be available to others in the network and should inform the work of the entire network. Making the learning of one educator or team available to and usable by other team members requires intentional facilitation and structured processes by the network's hub or central leadership group.[47] By directly supporting collaborative learning, continuous improvement can benefit a wide network of schools.[48]

CHAPTER 3

Component 1: RAPID CHECK-INS

Building Connections with Caring Adults

Intentional interactions between educators and students is at the heart of Personalization for Academic and Social-Emotional Learning (PASL). As described in chapter 2, one core theme that emerged from the initial design work of the district PASL team was the assignment of educator teams to follow a cohort of students over their high school careers. As this theme was further developed, rapid check-ins became the first intentional point of contact in this mentoring relationship. Teachers conduct rapid check-ins—a deliberate conversation—with each student in their designated class over a set time. The conversations range from short informal discussions to more exploratory, in-depth questions about a student's academic progress and social life. Through these conversations, adults show interest in and caring for students while also noting how the student is doing. At first glance, an adult's check-in with a student might look like any normal teacher-student interaction. Yet rapid check-ins are intentional, with features that make the interaction meaningful. Through these interactions, students and adults build a relationship that is mutually beneficial.

As one of the original three pilot groups in Broward County Public Schools, the team at Blanche Ely High School was instrumental in helping pilot, revise, and define what rapid check-ins entailed. Cherie Hodgson-Toeller, the Ely intern principal, led the school's PASL team as the members decided how to organize rapid check-ins in their school. Despite a local community that strongly identifies with Ely High School and its long history, the school also faced an imperative to improve student attendance. With this in mind, the school PASL team organized its reform activities around the first period of the day, calling it the Power of Period One. For students, their first-period teacher became their PASL teacher. Power of Period One teachers conducted rapid check-ins and goal-achievement lessons (see chapter 4), integrating them into their daily habits and routines. With strong leadership from the original district PASL team, the school team members embraced PASL and were excited to share it with the rest of the school. They saw rapid check-ins as the building block and built their PASL program from there.

As the team began its implementation of the reforms, Hodgson-Toeller gave every teacher a binder with PASL-related tabs. She provided attendance sheets and "little friendly colorful reminders about the expectations" to make the tasks "less imposing." For rapid check-ins, each teacher had a sheet for documenting the interactions with each student in the class. As another administrator explained, "We provided everyone with a template. The actual simplified idea was to increase the communication between you and students on an individual basis, and we are doing that." The teachers noted each check-in with each student in their first-period class. Hodgson-Toeller explained that the sheet "started as a compliance tool," but as teachers saw its value and as the PASL reform grew at the high school, "they saw it as a way to go, 'Oh, aha, you know I need to check in with this kid. They're slipping through the cracks.' Or, 'You know when I haven't been checking in with them, I've seen the decline in their attendance or their grades.'" When asked about their use of rapid check-ins in the second year of implementation, 37 percent of the teachers reported conducting them more than once a week, 29 percent said they checked in once a week, and the remainder said they conducted the check-ins within the four-week school expectation.

As discussed earlier, the teachers experimented with different approaches and used the PDSA cycle to gather evidence on what was working and to improve their rapid check-ins. Originally, the teachers decided to keep track of their check-ins on a physical attendance sheet. After the first PDSA cycle, the teachers realized that merely noting the check-in did not provide enough information to track students who were experiencing larger issues. During the second cycle, they implemented a clearer way to identify the students who needed resources such as a check-in with a counselor, denoting students who voiced concerns about their grades or home issues. At the end of each nine-week grading period, Hodgson-Toeller checked each PASL teacher's binders. While this review was framed as a way for the administration to help teachers with their implementation, it also helped make the teachers accountable.

In the second year of implementation, teachers were given a PASL binder that was more of a resource and less of an accountability tool. In addition to the sheets that teachers could use at their discretion to track students, it also included tabs with activities for goal achievement as well as general social-emotional learning lessons that teachers were encouraged to use if they had down time in class.

The teachers abandoned the formal check-in sheet so that they had autonomy to keep track of students in their own way. In so doing, the teachers adapted the rapid check-ins to their own individual and group needs, rather than implementing the check-ins as a uniform practice overseen by the administration. Although autonomy won over formal accountability, the teachers described meeting informally to discuss a student and then monthly in a PASL professional learning community (PLC) meeting to discuss student progress. One teacher explained: "We come together for the students, but then we all talk about . . . who we're having issues with. And it's good, because we can finally just talk to each [other], and it's like building relationships. I mean, I've talked more to Ms. Cornelius and Ms. Martinez this year than I have in the twelve years we've been working together. Which is great."[1] Teachers developed shared accountability over students' progress during their discussions in PLC meetings, enjoying the collegiality along the way.

During our interviews, teachers described developing their own methods for checking in with students. An English teacher explained that she did rapid check-ins "very easily": "I'd go around the room; they wouldn't even know I was doing a check-off. I would just walk around, and then I'd come back and I'd check off my list. And if there was somebody else that I needed to see how they were, then I did that." Another teacher, in contrast, reported that she had every student come to her desk during seatwork at least once a week: "I had them on my desk one by one. 'Okay, you have three Fs. Why do you have three Fs? Okay, is there anything that I could do to help? Do you understand the classes? Do you need extra tutoring?'" She said she had been taught to do this sort of personal interaction during her training as a nationally board-certified teacher, so the rapid check-ins made sense to her. A modern-language teacher said that she focused on a fourth of the class each week, asking students about their extracurricular activities, athletics, and musical interests. As the process was adopted at the school, a teacher explained that he did not like checking off the form in front of a student, saying it "depersonalized" the interaction. Instead, this teacher made sure to interact with each student and to note it afterward. As long as teachers were documenting their check-ins and referring students who needed extra attention, it did not matter how the adults integrated the interaction into their daily dealings with students. They were free to adapt their check-ins in whatever way they felt most comfortable.

Although the teachers tended to focus more on students' academic progress, a few described how the rapid check-ins helped them increase their awareness of students' social and emotional status. The check-ins encouraged the adults to see students more holistically, allowing them to still keep an eye on academics while also adding a personal touch. One teacher said, "I really started thinking about the student more as a person than I did as a just-doing-the-academic part. I think that really helped me try to create these relationships with students. That's what I really like about [PASL] . . . getting to know your students." Another teacher explained: "I look at PASL as more as a personal association with my students than, 'Okay, this young man has this learning disability. All right, let me help him out.' I kind of like to look at it as I'm trying to connect personally with this student, and whatever we can achieve out of that connection, that personal connection, if it has to do with academic stuff, then that's kind of like a cherry on top. Like, that's a bonus, that's a plus. I think it's—I look at PASL again as something that it's more personal than an academic focus, even though obviously it's something that needs to be or could be academic driven. But I think that personalization part will be helpful for them to feel comfortable in an academic setting."

Students at Ely High School described different ways that their Power of Period One teachers interacted with them. The teens did not seem to think of teachers as intentionally checking in with them, but described their first-period teachers as attentive. In a focus group of ninth graders we interviewed, students gave multiple examples of how their teachers interacted with them. They explained that teachers asked them about academics, helped identify a summer camp consistent with their interests, and identified an online Japanese language program for a girl obsessed with manga. One student explained: "Ms. Green helps me, like, stay focused, because she sees my potential and she knows that I set high standards for myself. So, she'll talk to my teachers and arrange for certain things . . . since I want to be a pediatrician and it's in the medical field."[2] Another student said that she appreciated when a teacher incorporated stories from her own life: "from something that happened to her, so we kind of understand the story better."

Students also described teachers as providing encouragement and support. "When she realized that I was, like, playing around and not being focused," one student said about a chemistry teacher, "she pulled me to the side and told me to stay focused and that I have potential." Another student said of his teacher, "He's always giving these motivational speeches that always, like, gives you high hopes and helps you stay above." Another student explained: "One teacher helped me was when I used to constantly come to school late, and she used to get on me like she was my mom, but I respected that. And she used to tell me, 'You have to be on time so you can get certain grades, so you can get out of high school,' . . . and ever since then, I done improved that since her encouragement, words."

The adults at Ely High School appreciated the intentionality brought by rapid check-ins. They also described how the check-ins served as a jumping-off point to other practices. Because the Power of Period One teachers also conducted goal-achievement lessons, these teachers could link their students' interests and goals with their check-ins. The teachers said that before the PASL effort, they had been checking in with students through quarterly "data chats," where they reviewed each student's grades, test scores, and attendance, but that the rapid check-ins helped make these chats more intentional. Teachers also said that the data chats had tended to focus on students' academic progress and that the rapid check-ins and Cross-Talks helped broaden the focus to students' social-emotional and behavioral needs.

Why Rapid Check-Ins?

Studies show that high school students often feel disconnected from school and alienated there.[3] As they navigate through academic expectations, friend dynamics, demanding and stressed teachers, and their own general anxiety, the teens need adults who acknowledge and care about them. Teachers' clear demonstration that they care about students can have powerful results. Even small acts of attention, kindness, and concern have important social-emotional payoffs in relationship building and communication skills.[4] When adolescents enter high school, they often lose some self-esteem and feel disconnected and lonely.[5] There are ways, however, that schools can stem this loss of self-esteem. When students feel a sense of belonging at their school, they are more likely to attend classes and perform better in them.[6] Through their interactions with students, teachers help students have trust in their school community. And this sense of trust is a proven advantage for both adults and students inside and outside the classroom.[7]

Adults in schools interact and show students they care in many ways. As part of the typical school day, adults connect with students about grades, attendance, assignments, and other general expectations. Adults can also take interest in students' athletic and other extracurricular activities related to school. For example, they might comment on an article in the school newspaper or the successes of the volleyball team. They also communicate with students more informally. Teachers share their love of their academic subject with students. They motivate students to perform well on assignments, appealing to the students' desire to learn the skills and knowledge of the subject matter. Other adults connect with students around common areas of interest such as sports, television shows, or current events. A few adults tell stories about their own family life or pets to relate with students. Not only are these different ways of communicating good for students as the teens learn to interact with adults, but the interactions also build a foundation of interest and trust as adults show students that they care about the adolescents' success both in and out of school.

These interactions establish and maintain healthy, constructive adult-student relationships inside and outside the classroom.[8] As psychology professor Rebecca McHugh and her colleagues explain, building strong, caring relationships or practicing "effortful engagement" between adults and students is when "one person actively and deliberately engages another on an interpersonal level."[9]

Plenty of research supports the importance of these interactions. Strong relationships between a student and an adult have been repeatedly found to be central to the success of resilient children.[10] Social cognitive theory suggests that when adults show interest in and caring for students, they engage in practices that increase students' noncognitive skills, including self-efficacy, sense of belonging, and development of personal agency. These skills, in turn, improve students' academic and behavioral outcomes. Students who feel that they can pursue their interests, realize their potential, and are supported by adults in the school are more likely to feel self-confident or believe in their capacities to exercise self-control and self-determination. When students feel greater self-efficacy, they are also more likely to take responsibility for their behavior and future life circumstances.[11] These types of deliberate efforts shape students' sense of belonging.[12]

Adults in schools also benefit from their positive, constructive relationships with students. Studies have found that teachers are typically intrinsically motivated and find meaning through their work with students.[13] Teacher enthusiasm has been associated with positive outcomes, including student achievement and student interest and persistence.[14] Through their interactions with students, teachers obtain important information that can inform their instructional decisions and build their students' enthusiasm about the subject matter. Teachers who use strategies that draw on students' language, culture, and lived experiences have been found to have more engaged students.[15]

Structuring a time for adults and students to interact in school in a nonacademic context is not a new idea. Homerooms and advisories have been a feature of high schools for many decades. In homerooms, teachers serve primarily as a point person at the school, handing out important school information such as progress reports and report cards. Studies have found that students who attend schools with homerooms have a higher sense of belonging in their school. As education researcher Becky Smerdon explains, this positive outcome is the result of the schools' providing "students with regular adult contact outside the typical teacher-student interaction and promot[ing] positive relationships between students and their teachers."[16]

Advisories are other official school periods that are not designed for academics per se. Vincent Anfara, professor at the University of Tennessee, Knoxville, describes advisories as structured times in schools "predicated on the beliefs that every young adolescent should have at least one adult at school to act as an advocate and that advisories help young adolescents navigate a challenging developmental stage of life."[17] These meeting times can have several goals, such as building community between and among students and their teachers, as well as developing social-emotional or academic skills.[18] Advisories have also been associated with a reduction in the number of dropouts.[19] And they have been connected with improvements in prosocial skills, students' sense of self-worth, and student-teacher relationships.[20]

Other approaches aim to structure the adult-student relationship even further. Coming out of dropout prevention and behavior management programs, these efforts directly match one student with one adult in the school in the effort to build prosocial and proactive behavior. The Check & Connect program is one example. The program, endorsed by the What Works Clearinghouse and aimed at reducing dropout numbers, has been found to increase students' progression and retention in school.[21] Check & Connect is predicated on the idea that adults and students will build relationships that will lead to "mutual trust and open communication," which, in turn, leads to "a persistent source of academic motivation, a continuity of familiarity with the youth and family, and a consistency in the message that 'education is important for your future.'"[22] Students in Check & Connect programs are three to four times more likely to increase their attendance than are other students, and the program participants showed an improvement in academic performance and a reduction in referrals.[23] During the check-ins, the adult clarifies behavioral expectations with the student and provides feedback and positive reinforcement.[24] Through this "non-contingent attention," students have an adult whom they can rely on in school and who is keeping track of them.[25]

Features of Rapid Check-Ins

At its core, the rapid check-in is a conversation between a teacher and each student in the teacher's class over a set period, such as two or three weeks. During this time, the teacher checks in with each student. For the majority of students, the interaction will be a brief conversation. As the year goes by, the teacher will know to ask the basketball player about his or her last game, the student government leader about the upcoming pep rally, or the student who works at Dunkin Donuts about the store's new offerings. Through humor and curiosity, teachers let each student know that they see and are interested in him or her. This goes both for the student who naturally comes to the teacher's desk to give an update on a movie seen over the weekend and for the student who sits in the back of the class and has figured out how to never speak to adults.

While most rapid check-ins are routine, the teacher can also have exploratory conversations when there are concerns raised by a student's grades, attendance, or general behavior. Here, teachers check in with the teen to delve into the root cause of behavior that raises concerns about the students' academic status, social-emotional state, and behavior. Teachers may ask why a student has seemed tired or disconnected. They might also probe why a student has had three days of absences or has been chronically late. These conversations help solve a problem or open a pathway to other support services offered by the school through the counselor, assistant principal, or school social worker.

Rapid check-ins ensure that a teacher is assigned to a set of students and will formally and regularly check in with them. As with other components of PASL, each school designs its own approach to rapid check-ins according to its own circumstances and needs. There is both structure and flexibility in rapid check-ins.

Schools need to make three decisions as they implement rapid check-ins and adapt them to their situation. First, schools must identify the adults who will be assigned to a group of students, optimally between twenty and twenty-five teens. Some schools decide to assign all teachers during a certain period of the day, such as Power of Period One or second period, because it often has the highest attendance. If check-ins are conducted by a classroom teacher who also grades the student, the teacher has a sense of how the student is doing academically. The teacher can therefore draw on this information as the year progresses. This approach also has the benefit of all students during that time having a PASL teacher.

Other schools, however, elect to conduct the rapid check-ins during a homeroom period or an advisory class. In Broward County, some schools call these homerooms *personalization periods*. While teachers in these homerooms may not have the student in one of their academic classes, the homeroom approach has the advantage of offering the student a relationship with an adult who does not have them in an evaluative context. In this way, the PASL teacher is not constrained by an academic curriculum and has the time and space to implement other content during this period. We have seen teachers use this time to bring in guest speakers, do mindfulness activities, and show videos on a number of subjects.

Finally, we have seen a third approach, in which schools target certain departments or teachers, particularly if they focus on a smaller subgroup of students such as low performing students. When personalization is done this way, the school identifies teachers who it sees as skilled at making connections and places them with this group of students.

Another decision that schools need to make is how teachers will record their rapid check-ins and how this information will be shared with other adults. In the same way that they make lesson plans, preparing and sharing their upcoming instructional procedures, PASL teachers are accountable for keeping track of their PASL students through a rapid check-in log. In these logs, they note whether everything is fine with a student or if the student needs extra school resources or other follow-up. Teachers tell us that this act of documentation transforms "something we are doing anyway" to a systematic act that makes sure no student in the class is missed. How teachers record their rapid check-ins has implications for teacher accountability.

One approach is for teachers to have a physical PASL binder containing their student roster and check-off boxes. Under this system, teachers denote their interactions with students with the date of the interaction and share the sheets only if asked. Another approach is to have a centralized online system. Here, teachers have a common online document or program in which they record their comments and concerns. Because it is online, the document is available to other teachers, counselors, and administrators if they have a question about a student or want to keep track of multiple students. Each school develops its own set of parameters for what teachers will include in the online forms, deciding on information such as involvement in extracurricular activities and goal setting. Some schools have teachers color-code the students according to risk (e.g., green for students needing no extra services, yellow for students potentially at-risk, and red for those clearly at-risk). This approach is particularly helpful for assistant principals and counselors trying to identify and assist students who are struggling academically or in other areas. The color coding makes it easier to spot students in need of extra attention and to understand if other teachers have concerns about the student.

Finally, schools have to decide if they will share this routine with students or keep the practice part of a teacher's routine, much like how a student may not know about a lesson plan and a teacher's discretion to adapt it. Informing students that teachers are connecting with them through a rapid check-in process lets students know that these connections are a priority for the teacher and the school. Knowing about the process can help the students feel that there is an adult in the school who is designated to be there for them, assist them when they need help, and lead them to appropriate resources. Teachers can also decide, however, to make rapid check-ins less overt. Some teachers want their check-ins with students to feel organic; they worry that making the documentation known to students erodes what needs to feel like a natural relationship. Both approaches are options, and the school and individual teacher need to decide how they want to proceed.

Broward County schools have experimented with different approaches to make the documentation authentic to teachers' daily instruction and tasks. Ultimately, each school and teacher will choose which approach best fits their teachers, counselors, assistant principals, and students. There are no wrong decisions, just a set of choices and directions.

A common misconception about rapid check-ins is that teachers are moving into the role of counselor, social worker, or therapist. We sometimes hear concerns that doing this kind of work involves an emotional investment that teachers consider not part of their work. High school teachers often see themselves as content specialists, for example, in algebra or world history, and do not see their role as getting involved in students' lives beyond their classrooms.[26] We suggest that each teacher, therefore, needs to develop his or her own approach to rapid check-ins, with the recognition that some teachers will connect with students through their academic relationships, while other teachers may feel comfortable delving more into students' social lives. Either approach is fine as the teacher establishes an authentic way to check in with students. Furthermore, schools have adults—counselors, administrators, and social workers—whose job is to help students with personal concerns. The responsibility of helping the student get access to this support, however, can fall to the classroom teacher.

Adapting and Scaling Rapid Check-Ins

Coconut Creek High School is located about ten minutes away from Blanche Ely High School. With an enrollment of approximately fourteen hundred students, Coconut Creek is on the smaller side of Broward County high schools. It has similar demographics to Ely, with approximately 75 percent of students qualifying for free and reduced-price lunch and 74 percent identifying as African American, 14 percent identifying as Latinx, and 9 percent White or Asian. The school's mission is to "educate students in a safe learning environment, maximizing each student's potential, through the use of specific and targeted academic and career-oriented programs." The large 1970s-style concrete building that constitutes the school was under-enrolled when we visited during the 2015–2016 school year.

As a school that started adopting PASL reforms in the scale-out phase, Coconut Creek benefited from learning about the experiences of the three pilot schools. The school PASL team decided to focus on the entire ninth grade, monitoring all the students' grades and attendance records. Special attention, however, was given to students who had a GPA of 2.0 or lower—more than half of the ninth graders; teachers followed up with these students and let them know about tutoring opportunities.

The teachers met every other Thursday in the office of the ninth-grade administrator to discuss students' progress, particularly those deemed at-risk. Judith Segesta, who was also head of the school's PASL team, described PASL as important for students: "Because our students in this day and age need a lot more connections, personal connections, one-on-one with humans, not social media. So they actually need to learn how to accept conversations and interactions with adults. We have a different society where it's not as accepting as usual because of social media. So this is a great opportunity for people to connect, and human interaction is the upmost key to success for students to learn."

Because of their focus on student connections, the teachers emphasized rapid check-ins as a core activity. Indeed, in our interviews with the school's ninth-grade teachers, we found that the teachers generally embraced rapid check-ins. Of the twenty teachers we interviewed, six reported that they checked in more than once a week, seven teachers said once a week, and the rest said at least once a month.

Teachers at Coconut Creek had a firm grasp of the different steps of rapid check-ins, including the intentional discussions, the focus on academics and social-emotional aspects of a student's life, and the documentation of the interaction. They were generally enthusiastic about rapid check-ins, understanding their value. As a teacher explained, "It's just a way to connect with your students, but at a more formal approach, I guess. More—how do y'all say?—direct. You know, you're doing it, and you're writing it down, so it's a way of gathering information on your students and familiarizing yourself with your students." Similarly, an adult who teaches intensive reading described the check-ins as "making the personal connection so that they feel they can come to you and they know that you care, so that they're not just one of the many kids there."

Interestingly, teachers described different approaches for documentation. One teacher said it was difficult to keep records, referring to the practice as "paperwork." An algebra teacher described the challenges related to consistency. He said that he tried to "keep a good record of the students" but that sometimes, record keeping was difficult with the demands of math instruction: "You know, [students] give me their feedback, how's everything at home, and things that they're struggling with, because sometimes they probably need some advice in certain things. Whatever it is that I can help [with], I help. If I can't handle it, I will refer them to the counselor to deal with it."

Another teacher talked about coordinating the rapid check-ins with data chats the teacher had held with students about their quarterly grades and attendance. Like the teacher at Ely High School, another said that it didn't feel authentic to tell students that he was checking in with them explicitly. Instead, he waited until the end of the period to make his notes. One teacher captured the general philosophy at Coconut Creek: "The better that you connect with the students, the easier it is for you when you design your lessons, and you know what certain students are going with, and it could help you better serve them."

All the ninth-grade students at Coconut Creek could identify a teacher who they could talk to. One student put it this way: "We don't have teachers that want to see us fail. They want to help us get us to college and stuff. So they stay late. If we need make up work, they give it to us." Other students explained that teachers showed they cared when they made sure that the students did their work and when the adults pulled the teens aside to do makeup work. One teen said, "When I'm failing, they tell me to come after school so they could help me." In addition to receiving academic monitoring and advising, students also described going to teachers when they were upset or had family problems. A student talked about a time he had gotten into a fight. The teacher had sat down with him until he calmed down. Another teacher made her room available for supplies for projects for other courses. When asked, most of the students had not been referred to the school counselor, but they agreed that if they had to go, a teacher would not hesitate to refer them.

Taken together, the adults and teachers at both Blanche Ely High School and Coconut Creek High School embraced rapid check-ins as a valuable approach to helping the students in their school and classroom. Each adult adapted the check-in practice to his or her own style and approach, and all the adults understood the importance of tracking students and following up with assistance and resources, if need be.

Conclusion

As we studied this core element of PASL, we found that adults and students respond positively to rapid check-ins. Educators welcome the practice as something consistent with their understanding of their work. Teachers appreciate that they can adapt the practice to their own personal style. They also acknowledge its power to engage students in their class. Schools and teachers adapt rapid check-ins to their own conceptions of accountability and autonomy. Whether the check-ins are documented with paper and binders, as at Ely High School, or through a digital system like the one described above, schools see the value of check-ins. Although each school must decide how it will adapt rapid check-ins to its own environment, evidence suggests that the check-ins are an important way to help high school students feel valued and heard.

In the broader context of PASL, rapid check-ins represent a building block in this reform. Not only do they embody the importance of relationships inherent in PASL, but they also represent the core activity in the system of personalization. From the rapid check-in, teachers learn about students' interests and lives to support goal-achievement lessons. And when teachers refer to student data for additional information, they further improve their interactions with the students. Rapid check-ins that are complemented with data such as attendance and grades can thus help teachers identify students who need additional resources, for example, from an assistant principal or a guidance counselor. Teachers also draw on their rapid check-ins when they meet in educator teams to discuss student progress. Finally, rapid check-ins promote a culture of personalization by demonstrating to students that adults are interested in them, willing to reach out, and will follow through with questions or concerns.

CHAPTER 4

Component 2: GOAL SETTING AND ACHIEVEMENT

Explicit Teaching of Social-Emotional Skills

Western High School, as its name implies, sits on the western side of Broward County, not far from the entrance to the Everglades. The school opened in 1981 in the fast-growing town of Davie, which itself was developed by filling in the waterlogged outskirts of the Everglades. With over thirty-one hundred students, Western is currently the fourth-largest high school in Broward County. The student population is about 43 percent White and 42 percent Latinx, with small percentages of students who are Black, Asian, Native American, or multiracial. About 42 percent of the students are economically disadvantaged. Western High School typically earns high grades on the state's accountability system and offers a variety of AP courses; an advanced curriculum in robotics, rocketry, and biotechnology; and dual-enrollment programs. Principal Jimmy Arrojo describes the environment as "big school, small family," which reflects his goal of having each student and staff member feel safe, included, and respected in the school.

Mariana is a ninth grader at Western.[1] Her experience reflects those of many students at the school. More than one family member has been in trouble with the law for drug or gang-related offenses. When asked about her career plans, Mariana says she wants to go into law enforcement as a way to end the cycle she sees in her family and to make her mother, who is raising her as a single parent, proud of her. Like many students her age, she spends a lot of time on social media. The digital world offers a way to connect with her friends, but it also can be a place where her friends say mean things. While Mariana does not seek out fights, she has a quick temper when the conversation takes a bad turn, and these disagreements can spill over into face-to-face interactions.

Around mid-October, Mariana arrived in her personalization class and saw that the assistant principal, Derek Gordon, would be leading the class instead of the regular teacher. At the start of the class, Gordon began to talk about goals. Through this lesson, Mariana learned about the qualities of effective goals, how to set clear and measurable goals, and how short-term goals work toward longer-term goals. Gordon encouraged the students to set goals that were related to their interests and abilities, were important to them, and were clear and observable. Mariana learned the acronym SMART—specific, measurable, attainable, relevant, and timely—as characteristics of good goals. When Gordon asked the students about their goals, one student replied, "I want to be famous." Gordon replied that he recognized that many students had big dreams. "But goals are different from dreams," he said. "Goals are more specific and actionable. Goals are about developing the skills that will help you get to where you want to go." He continued with an example: "Being famous or having your own band is not a very effective goal. A better goal is to play the guitar well enough to be able to join a band." Gordon gave an example of the steps a student might take if he or she wanted to play the guitar well enough to join a band and the support the student might seek out to get there.

Gordon then told the story of Jon Feliciano. Mariana was intrigued to learn that a Western High School graduate was now playing for the Oakland Raiders. She watched the video with interest, learning that despite starting life with a foot deformity and leg braces, Feliciano set a goal early in life to attend the University of Miami. When he entered Western, Feliciano realized that football was his path to college, and he learned to play. He stayed in school despite encountering substantial family challenges, ultimately earning a football scholarship to the University of Miami. Feliciano was the first in his family to graduate from college, and he went on to reach his goal of playing professional football. After the students watched the video about Feliciano, Gordon asked them to think about what they had just seen and to read the ESPN article that had some additional details about Feliciano's path to the University of Miami. Mariana and her classmates then filled in a worksheet as if they were Feliciano. What goals did the football player set? What steps did he take? What obstacles did he encounter?

After the class discussed Feliciano's story and his goals, Gordon had the students write down their own goals, and he then asked for a few examples. Mariana talked about her goal to become a police officer. After applauding her for having a clear career interest, he said, "Remember, good goals are specific and actionable. How can we break that down into steps you can take now?" Mariana was unsure. Gordon then asked, "Do you know what types of grades you need to get into the police academy? What type of physical tests do you need?" Mariana responded that she didn't know and was not sure how to find that out. Gordon replied, "We have a school resource officer who is on campus every day. Talk with her about what it takes to be a police officer. Her sergeant from the Davie police department is here once a month. Talk with him about what it takes to get into the police academy."

Gordon saw Mariana's eyes widen with the recognition that becoming a police officer involved many steps and selective admission criteria. He decided to tell the class a story about a student who was in his office and said she wanted to be a pediatrician. As he usually did when he met with students, Gordon looked up the student's grades and saw she was failing biology. He asked the class, "How is the student on the path to be a pediatrician if she is failing biology in high school? You may be fourteen years old now, but what you do in high school is putting you on a path for your future." Gordon then referred back to Mariana. "If you want to be a police officer," he said, "you can work toward that goal right now in high school, but you have to know the steps to get there." He offered to call the school resource officer for her and make the introduction.

A few weeks later, Mariana met with the school resource officer in Gordon's office. The officer spent a few minutes talking with Mariana about her job as a police officer and how to be admitted to the police academy. Unfortunately, this was not the only time Mariana visited Gordon's office. Although she came on her own this time, she was later sent there a couple times for misbehavior stemming from her quick temper. Each time she was sent to the office, Gordon talked with her about her grades and her goal to become a police officer.

He later told us about these conversations: "Our approach to discipline is not just to send students to internal suspension, but to connect with students and help them find the right path." With Mariana, Gordon continued to ask her if she was making progress on her career goal.

Because of Gordon's introduction, Mariana soon developed a relationship with the school resource officer. Gordon would see them talking after school, when students were still milling around the campus. Mariana later said that the officer became a mentor and was someone she could go to when she found her temper getting the best of her. Mariana began to take control of her temper. Her grades improved and she is making progress on her goal to be a police officer.

A Curriculum for Goal Achievement

When PASL became the focus of our partnership with Broward County Public Schools, goal setting and goal achievement were not discussed in the report that defined PASL. Yet the lessons oriented around goal achievement and related skills that Western High School used to help Mariana achieve her career goal emerged to be a core element of PASL. In the design phase, the district PASL team assessed various needs and learned about specific practices to integrate students' academic and social-emotional learning experiences. Through this process, the explicit teaching of academic and social-emotional skills emerged as one of the three major themes for infusing PASL practices across the schools.

As the work shifted into the development phase, the working group tasked by the district PASL team to develop the PASL curriculum heard from focus groups of teachers who had been implementing a related curriculum. After receiving this input, the group became focused on the challenges of implementation. The implementing teachers struggled to find time to incorporate all the lessons. To make this even more difficult, the district was also rolling out a new teacher evaluation instrument, and the working group wanted to ensure the teacher behaviors expected for the evaluation did not conflict with modeling social-emotional skills.

Ultimately, the working group recommended focusing on a subset of lessons that were most closely aligned with PASL's goals and the new teacher evaluation and that had a strong base of research behind them. In light of the working group's review of the research on how to develop social-emotional competencies and in support of district priorities, we decided to focus the curriculum on goal achievement. Activities around goal achievement included helping students set goals, develop an action plan, and then monitor their progress toward their goals, as well as helping students cope with emotions, handle stress, and manage relationships.

Research on Goal Achievement

The district PASL team's decision to focus on goal achievement in developing students' social-emotional competencies was based on several factors. First, substantial research demonstrates the power of setting goals and monitoring progress for self-regulation.[2] Goal-achievement skills contribute to improved academic performance and self-regulation because these skills can direct your attention, effort, and action toward an objective. Second, goals are critical to two of the five social-emotional learning competencies—self-awareness and self-management—that are promoted by the Collaborative for Academic, Social, and Emotional Learning, an evidence-based organization for promoting social-emotional learning.[3] Together, self-awareness and self-management focus on your ability to know your current status and adjust your behavior to reach goals.

Third, goal setting and monitoring improve student outcomes because they motivate the student and develop their cognitive skills and self-regulation. The motivational and cognitive power of goal setting can be seen through the mottos "Work harder" and "Work smarter." In this way, goals help students to work harder and smarter. When they self-regulate, students monitor whether they are achieving their desired learning outcomes, and if not, they will change their behavior or strategy to improve their learning. Indeed, self-regulation theory connects the proactive learning processes of goal setting to outcomes such as grades and academic achievement. Overall, the research indicates that goal-achievement skills play a critical role in integrating the academic and social-emotional aspects of learning.[4]

Goal-achievement skills and motivation mutually reinforce each other. A goal orientation shapes motivation in class, and motivation leads to a student's setting more specific and harder goals. For example, a study found that making progress on a goal led to higher self-efficacy, which led to a person's aiming even higher.[5] When students attain their goals, they set higher ones in the future and experience positive emotions such as a sense of accomplishment, pride, joy, and general well-being. Goal-achievement interventions may be particularly important for students from less advantaged backgrounds, who tend to have lower academic and interpersonal expectations, exhibit fewer self-regulatory behaviors, and demonstrate less goal commitment.

Substantial research indicates that explicit training around goals can improve the types of objectives students set and their ability to make progress on them. For example, a longitudinal study of goal setting in twenty-three high schools found that involving students in setting short- and long-term learning goals and in tracking their own progress led to improved academic performance in language arts.[6] Another study showed that eleventh-grade students in a vocational education course exhibited more self-regulatory behaviors after engaging in a program designed to teach them how to set goals, develop a plan to achieve them, evaluate their progress, and adjust.[7] In short, many school-based interventions that involve students in setting goals and monitoring their progress are associated with improved self-regulation behaviors, academic performance, attendance, and behavior.

Key Features of Goal Achievement

The research on goal-achievement activities focuses not only on the positive outcomes of these interventions, but also on the key components that make these interventions work. The empirical research identifies three important features that support positive outcomes: setting mastery or learning goals, visualizing obstacles and ways to overcome them, and having opportunities for monitoring goal progress. Each of these elements was incorporated into the initial goal-achievement lessons.

Aiming Toward Mastery and Learning

Several studies on goal achievement have found that it is not just the presence of goals, but also their nature, that is important. Many people are familiar with the importance of SMART goals: those that are specific, measurable, attainable, relevant, and timely. Indeed, the research behind goal achievement supports the need for attainable goals. Those that are specific and challenging yet feasible are more likely to lead to greater effort and persistence than are vague or easy objectives.[8] Just telling students to do their best is not specific enough to guide their focus and motivate them to direct their action in a particular way. Yet the research on goal achievement also identifies an important aspect that is not obvious when we focus on the SMART acronym: the role of a mastery orientation. Goals that are oriented toward mastery (or learning) activate the mechanisms that connect goal setting to student outcomes by fostering motivation and metacognitive strategies.

Goal setting works because it focuses students' attention, and mastery-oriented goals focus their attention even better.[9] Goal theory highlights the importance of two major types of orientation. Some goals, referred to as *mastery or learning goals*, are oriented toward "increasing one's competency, understanding, and appreciation for what is being learned."[10] Others, known as *achievement or performance goals*, are oriented toward "outperforming others as a means to aggrandize one's ability status at the expense of peers."[11] In other words, mastery goals emphasize the content of what is being learned, while performance goals are focused on external indicators of achievement. When Gordon asked Mariana and her classmates about their goals, he distinguished between the "big dreams" students may have for what they want to achieve, such as being famous, and mastery-oriented goals that work on skills and understanding. Learning to play the guitar well enough to join a band reflects a mastery goal that helps build the underlying skills they need to be in a famous band.

Substantial research demonstrates the power of mastery or learning goals. For example, a study of secondary school students found that students who were motivated by mastery expended more effort, made more progress, and were more successful on college entrance exams than students who didn't set mastery goals.[12] Another longitudinal study of high school students found that a mastery orientation led to greater classroom engagement, higher achievement, and more psychological satisfaction than did a performance orientation.[13] A mastery goal orientation is also related to an incremental theory of learning (i.e., a growth mindset). When students think an ability is fixed, they are more likely to adopt performance goals to either demonstrate their ability or to avoid revealing a lack of ability. But when students see ability as incremental, they are more likely to adopt goals focused on learning and mastering new skills. Students with a mastery orientation also display greater interest in academic activities.[14]

The power of mastery goals, however, comes not from the overall amount of effort extended, but from how they shape cognitive processes. All types of goals involve motivational processes that facilitate engagement, but a mastery or learning orientation also facilitates cognitive strategies. These strategies include identifying the knowledge that the student needs, seeking assistance from others, and displaying greater comprehension. Metacognitive strategies are particularly important when individuals need to acquire new knowledge. Setting a mastery or learning goal "draws attention away from the end result" and toward "the discovery of effective task processes."[15] Individuals aiming at mastery thus have more focused attention and are better able to persist in the face of challenges than are individuals aimed at performance.[16]

Visualizing Obstacles and Planning to Overcome Them

A second important component of goal-achievement interventions is having students visualize potential obstacles and develop plans to overcome them. These visualization and planning exercises generate metacognitive strategies that help students achieve their goals. In goal-setting research, visualizing obstacles is known as *mental contrasting*, a strategy that has students contrast their desired future with reflections about potential obstacles to that future.[17] While educators often encourage students to think positively, research indicates that too much positive thinking can actually be detrimental to goal achievement. The power of goal setting comes not from wishful thinking around the big dreams that students have, but from connecting their dreams to the steps needed to attain those dreams and considering likely obstacles they will encounter.[18] Mental contrasting is exactly what Gordon did when he pressed Mariana to think about the admissions requirements to the police academy. Through this approach, students can distinguish between feasible goals and infeasible wishes. Mental contrasting strengthens the link between expectation and goal pursuit by forming associations between the desired future and current reality.[19] The mechanism behind this link is that the process of identifying obstacles in achieving the desired future works to "instill the energy to overcome hardships on the way to wish fulfillment."[20]

An important part of mental contrasting is developing plans to overcome the potential obstacles identified. These plans often take the form of if-then statements. For example, students can be supported in developing plans that specify "if situation A is encountered, then I will initiate behavior B to reach goal C."[21] By outlining these plans, students can learn to automatically respond with the goal-directed action when obstacles are actually encountered.[22] Empirical tests of goal-achievement interventions show the importance of visualizing potential obstacles and identifying plans to overcome them. For example, mental contrasting interventions have been shown to improve student GPA, attendance, and behavior.[23] In a study of a similar intervention on tenth-grade students, teens who visualized potential obstacles and planned solutions to those obstacles demonstrated more persistence in studying for the PSAT than did students not exposed to the intervention.[24]

Monitoring Goal Progress

Finally, the link between setting goals and higher achievement rests on the student's ability to monitor progress toward the objective and to adjust accordingly.[25] Thus, goal-achievement interventions should provide opportunities for students to assess their progress. As education researchers Barry Zimmerman and Dale Schunk explain, a core component of self-regulation is the ability to "monitor and assess their goal progress" and "adjust strategies better."[26] Empirically, teaching students about goal setting helped them self-monitor and adjust their behavior as they progressed toward the aim. For example, the Self-Regulation Empowerment Program developed by leading goal theory researchers and tested in middle school classrooms teaches students how to engage in a cyclical process of setting goals, self-recording their outcomes and processes, evaluating their goal attainment, and adjusting their learning processes. At the high school level, an intervention that had students set learning objectives and provide evidence of their progress toward them at the end of a curricular unit led to higher student achievement. Across settings, the self-monitoring of progress toward goals is associated with goal achievement and improved outcomes.

Goal-setting research supports the popular SMART model. Mastery goals have some of the features of SMART goals: they are specific, achievable, and relevant. Less obviously, they also include both short and long-term goals. Establishing short-term goals supports a mastery goal orientation because they reflect the process necessary to achieve a longer-term goal.[27] Short-term feedback allows a student or another person to monitor their progress toward more distant goals. Goal-achievement theory, then, emphasizes the need for SMART-ER goals. That is, goal setting activates metacognitive processes, namely, the ability to *evaluate* progress and *revise* plans to achieve goals. Short-term monitoring of progress and adjusting strategies to achieve more distant goals also supports a mastery orientation because these steps focus on the strategies needed to attain goals and not just on outcomes.[28]

A comprehensive review of the implications of goal-setting research for the design of learning environments emphasizes the importance of monitoring progress, getting feedback, and outlining subprocesses in pursuit of larger goals.[29] Effective activities should enable students to get feedback on their work and collaborate with peers to identify the steps necessary to achieve goals. Importantly, the monitoring and feedback should not just focus on the overall goal, but should also consider the tasks that contribute to it. Learning environments that support goal achievement also embed reminders for students to recognize progress toward a goal (not just success at achieving a goal) and to celebrate that progress.

Helpful information on goal progress can come from many sources besides self-monitoring; external feedback can also be helpful.[30] For example, a study of a goal-achievement intervention in the eleventh grade found that having students view other students' goals, share ideas toward achieving these goals, and encourage each other through feedback supported the development of student self-regulation behaviors.[31] Another study found that in addition to goal setting, feedback from teachers improved students' writing achievement and self-efficacy.[32] Positive feedback on goal progress not only helps with goal achievement, but also facilitates a positive emotional reaction in students, such as increased interest, pride, and joy in learning.[33]

Piloting Goal-Achievement Lessons

The next step of developing PASL's goal-achievement activities was to test the lessons in the three pilot schools. The lessons were divided into five parts: (1) goal setting, (2) action planning and monitoring progress, (3) managing emotions and decision-making, (4) handling stress, and (5) managing relationships.

The first two lessons aimed to help students set clear, observable, and personally important goals; create action plans for each goal; identify supports and obstacles for each goal; and set and monitor benchmarks for success. As Mariana did with Gordon's guidance, students had to write a mastery goal and visualize its obstacles. However, rather than highlight the story of National Football

League player Jon Feliciano, the lesson used examples from famous historical figures who set goals. These examples included President John F. Kennedy's commitment to land on the moon within a decade, Marian Anderson's aspiration to be a singer, and Cesar Chavez's work to improve the conditions of migrant farm workers.

The key aims of the third, fourth, and fifth lessons were to help students learn to express their feelings in ways that produce positive outcomes and minimize negative ones. The lessons also taught students how to identify stressors, recognize the stress response and stress symptoms, and use coping strategies. Students also learned to accept other people's support and influence. While these skills are not directly related to goal achievement, they build other social-emotional skills the PASL team considered important.

As the pilot schools began implementation, they worked out the details of who would be involved and where the lessons would take place. One of the schools had a few Health Opportunities for Physical Education (HOPE) teachers on its team. The alignment of the goal-achievement skills with the HOPE curriculum, along with the packed curriculum in the core content areas, made the HOPE classes seem like a natural place for the lessons. The first lesson would be taught before the end of the second month of the school year, with the remaining lessons distributed over the year. Another school, which had no HOPE teachers on its PASL team, used the HOPE class period but had the counselor "push in" the lesson to avoid increasing the burden on HOPE teachers. In addition, all PASL teachers would receive professional development about the skills so they could reinforce the skills in other classes.

The major takeaways from the pilot goal-achievement lessons were the challenges of monitoring progress toward goals. For example, the students' goals were written on handouts that the teachers collected. These papers were easily misplaced, and there was no way to inform others in the school about the students' goals. When it came time to monitor progress toward their goals, students had often forgotten their action plans, and much of the process had to start over. As the three pilot schools shifted into the implementation phase, the goal-achievement lessons themselves stayed mostly the same, except for the introduction of an online platform for students to enter their goals. The school PASL coordinators could now download the student goals and share them with students' PASL teachers. The schools nevertheless still struggled with how often to work with students to monitor progress toward their goals.

Scaling: Bringing More Schools into the PASL Network

The following year saw a big change in PASL as the district began to scale the reform to new schools. In addition to the three pilot schools, five other high schools, known as scale-out schools, began participating in the PASL initiative. Among these five schools were Western High School and Pompano Beach High School.

WESTERN HIGH SCHOOL: A LOCAL HERO AS ROLE MODEL

Since the beginning of the design phase, Gordon had been an at-large member of the district PASL team. He was therefore involved in the initial design of the PASL innovation, even though his school was not one of the first to implement it. When Western High School was asked to join the network, Gordon had just been appointed its assistant principal. Naturally, he became the PASL coordinator. Gordon and the school's principal recruited five teachers to serve on the school's PASL team.

PASL reforms are designed to be adapted to the strengths, weaknesses, and other circumstances at each school. With that in mind, Gordon met with the school PASL team to make decisions about the goal-achievement lessons. He brought copies of the suggested lesson plans and other materials for each of the teachers on the team. After giving a brief summary of the materials he had distributed, Gordon was called away to deal with a pressing issue about a student.

In his absence, the team reviewed the goal-achievement materials. The teachers liked the basic approach of the first lesson, including the attention to the qualities of effective goals, developing an action plan, and visualizing obstacles. They were worried, however, about the use of historical figures as examples of goal achievement. While the list of individuals was diverse, the teachers thought that even someone like Cesar Chavez would seem more like a history lesson than someone personally engaging for the students. One teacher mentioned the story of Jon Feliciano, who had just been recently signed by the Oakland Raiders. The teachers agreed that a recent example of a student who came from their community and graduated from their school would be more successful at engaging students. They spent some time searching for resources about Feliciano to integrate into the lesson. When Gordon returned, the teachers told him about the changes they had made to the initial lesson. He was pleased with the progress they had made and the connection to their school community.

Western's PASL team made a few additional changes to the goal-achievement lessons. As they were all subject-area teachers, they decided to use fourth period for all their PASL activities. Using this dedicated time would support the integration of the goal-achievement lessons with other PASL components, such as rapid check-ins. Since the lessons would be taking time away from academic subjects, the teachers were concerned about the time needed for five separate lessons. They consequently streamlined the lessons to three, keeping much of the lesson material on monitoring goal progress and stress management.

Besides helping students monitor their progress toward the goals they had set in the first lesson, the PASL team also recognized that ninth graders are often unaware of how their GPA is calculated and why it is important. So, the team added a lesson on how the students could calculate their GPA. With the support of counselors, the team had students identify their stressors and their responses to this stress. The class also discussed time management and relaxation techniques. This lesson supported goal achievement by recognizing the emotional challenge of reaching toward a goal and by helping students develop effective emotional responses to these challenges. The PASL team also outlined when teachers would get professional development and the expectations for reinforcing the PASL skills beyond the discrete lessons.

POMPANO BEACH HIGH SCHOOL: INTEGRATING GOAL
ACHIEVEMENT AND PEER MENTORING

Pompano Beach High School also began implementing PASL as one of the first scale-out schools. This magnet school specializes in international affairs and information technology. With about twelve hundred students, it is on the smaller side for high schools in Broward County. The student population is about 50 percent White, 25 percent Black, and 25 percent Latinx. Slightly less than half of the students are economically disadvantaged. Pompano Beach has a well-developed student leadership program, hosting an international summit every year, with over 150 guests from countries all over the world. Like Western High School, Pompano Beach had strong administrative support, starting, importantly, with its principal, Hudson Thomas. During the first year of the school's implementation, Thomas explained, "I think there is a need for PASL because the students coming in need to have a feeling of belonging to the school and I think PASL plays an important part. Students need to feel that they're welcome and identify as being part of school." Another school administrator, Jill Samaroo, served on the district team that developed the core PASL components. Because of this involvement, Pompano Beach had a deep understanding of PASL when the school began planning its own implementation.

Western shared its revisions to the goal-achievement lessons, and Pompano Beach (and the rest of the PASL network) agreed that they were an improvement. Pompano Beach did make two important changes to its goal-achievement activities. First, rather than have counselors or teachers facilitate the goal-setting lesson in classrooms, the high school introduced students to the initial goal-setting lesson in a gradewide assembly led by teachers and peer mentors. Pompano Beach had an existing peer mentor program where higher-grade students met with ninth graders to discuss a variety of topics to ease the transition to high school. The school decided to use this structure to support PASL in general and goal achievement in particular. This adaptation illustrates how PASL emphasizes the ability to integrate new ideas, such as goal achievement, into existing school structures in ways that take advantage of current school strengths while building new opportunities for students.

The peer mentor relationship continues throughout the year, which relates to the second change that Pompano Beach made to the goal-achievement activities. Rather than limit instruction in goal monitoring and action planning to a single follow-up lesson, the school established a regular schedule where peer mentors, with teacher support, met with students every nine weeks to review their grades and progress toward their goals. During these interactions, students could develop additional action plans to achieve their goals, revise their current action plans if they were not making sufficient progress, or set new goals. This approach is also consistent with research findings that peers can be a valuable source of feedback when a person is monitoring progress toward goals.[34] At even more frequent intervals, about twice a month, the peer mentors led other types of activities that reflected the existing mentoring program. These activities tackled topics such as study skills and how to choose classes.

Districtwide Change: Introducing a Personalization Period

By the end of the scale-out year, eight high schools were part of the PASL network. The PASL skills, which were relatively undefined a short time previously, were coalescing around goal setting and monitoring, action planning, calculating GPA, and stress management. The next two years brought two important changes that were driven by larger districtwide changes. These districtwide initiatives forced each school to further adapt its goal-achievement activities.

One districtwide policy change was the introduction of a personalization period. There were many reasons for this initiative, but the implications for PASL's goal-achievement initiative were noteworthy. Before personalization periods were introduced, Broward County high schools had a traditional bell schedule. Students (and teachers) had the same classes each day, with roughly fifty-minute periods. Teachers had one planning period per day. After extensive negotiation with the teacher union, the district offered each school the option to adopt a block schedule. Faculty would vote on whether to make the change. The block schedule meant that students would only have four classes a day, each class for ninety minutes. The school schedule had an A day, with periods 1 through 4, and a B day, with periods 5 through 8. Teachers had a single ninety-minute planning period on one of those days. In addition, all students and teachers were assigned to a personalization period, which functioned much like a study hall. Teachers would take attendance but would otherwise not be required to do anything else during this time.

The personalization period created both opportunities and challenges for PASL's goal-achievement activities. One opportunity was the availability of a dedicated time and space for these activities. As the PASL implementation in both Western and Pompano Beach expanded to include all ninth graders, the personalization period offered teachers time to conduct goal-achievement activities with students in a way that did not compete with their subject-area curriculum or rely on HOPE classes, in which not all students had enrolled. The challenge was how to ensure teacher engagement without mandating teacher participation during the personalization period. With strong teacher support in Western and Pompano Beach, this challenge was less of a concern, and the personalization period was thus highly beneficial for PASL. The same teachers who were assigned to check in with students could also work with them to set and monitor goals. This arrangement fostered the integration and coordination of the PASL components. Although teachers initially struggled with communicating and documenting the students' goals, the new digital system made these tasks easier. Moreover, the integration of PASL with the personalization period allowed students to monitor their progress more often.

The other major district change was the introduction of Naviance, an online college and career counseling program that the district had purchased. Counselors were expected to have students use Naviance to explore careers and postsecondary opportunities. With Naviance's focus on goal setting, each school's PASL team had to figure out how the online program fit into the school's goal-achievement activities. Western tried to integrate Naviance into its existing activities by having the counselor conduct the second goal-achievement lesson. The counselor worked with students on their "final" goal in the same way that, as described earlier in the chapter, Gordon had helped Mariana refine hers. The counselor would then input this goal into Naviance and use this data as a starting point for further Naviance activities. Accessing the Naviance program, other teachers and staff could see what the students did, and the adults could refer to the data in their subsequent interactions with students.

Conclusion

We gained much insight about scaling up goal-achievement skills from our years of working with Broward County Public Schools. First, effective implementation at scale requires not just widely sharing some common practices, but also ensuring that those practices reflect the theory of action behind improving the students' outcomes. Our educator partners needed to deeply understand goal achievement and the beliefs surrounding it.[35]

In both Western and Pompano Beach's approach to goal achievement, there are common elements that reflect the underlying empirical research about goal achievement and student social-emotional competencies. Like other PASL components, goal achievement uses a shared set of PASL resources, tools, and artifacts that define each component. Students are first introduced to the nature of effective goals. They then set their own goals, develop an action plan, visualize obstacles to their goals, and monitor their progress over time. These lessons do more than bring consistency to how schools in the district implement goal achievement. They also emphasize the elements well documented as critical to goal-achievement interventions: a focus on mastery, or learning, goals; visualization of obstacles; and progress monitoring. Both Western and Pompano Beach High Schools also offered professional development about goal setting so that the teachers could become knowledgeable about the research on goal achievement, as we do in our network-wide meetings with the district. Yet improvement at scale requires attending to the systems and not just individuals. Our approach is both to build individual knowledge about the PASL practices and to develop systems, tools, and processes that support the desired student experience. Thus, the core elements of goal achievement are built into the shared lessons themselves.

A second aspect of scale is ownership, which is often a substantial challenge to scaling up educational innovations.[36] Our experience with goal achievement illustrates the importance of designing with, and for, the schools that will be implementing the innovation.[37] While the goal-achievement lessons were the core of the innovation, schools varied in how they adapted the lessons to reflect the unique context of the school. The presence of a recent Western alumnus who had just signed with the NFL provided a natural way to adapt the lessons to better connect with students at that school. As described in this chapter, Western's PASL team wanted the opportunity to revise the goal-achievement lessons to "make it their own." This phrase alone shows the power of codevelopment. While education often prioritizes teacher buy-in, it is teacher ownership that will lead to deeply embedded practices and long-term commitment to change. Ownership requires the ability to adapt to local circumstances.

Also important to ownership is the ability to integrate a reform into a school's existing priorities, needs, and strengths. Pompano Beach illustrates this form of integration with its peer mentoring program. The high school already had such a program, which it adapted to incorporate student peer mentors into the goal-achievement activities. Notably, this integration did not mean that PASL's goal-achievement activities and Pompano Beach's existing peer mentoring program were separate programs that coexisted. Instead, each effort was adapted to integrate with the other. Pompano Beach revised the "standard" PASL goal-achievement approach (while maintaining integrity to the core lessons) to include peer mentors. Likewise, the peer mentoring itself was revised to align with the expectations of goal-achievement activities. Pompano Beach represents a powerful example of adaptive integration, which is about using continuous improvement to bring a standard practice (goal-achievement lessons in this case) into a new context (e.g., a school with a strong history of peer mentoring).[38]

Beyond these two schools, we saw other examples of Broward County schools that have integrated goal achievement into their existing programs. Indeed, several other high school programs incorporate goal achievement as a natural way to integrate PASL into the school. The Junior Reserve Officer Training Corps (JROTC) and Advancement Via Individual Determination (a national college-readiness program) place a great emphasis on goal achievement and were present in many Broward County schools. Schools that had JROTC instructors on their PASL team, for example, found ways to align PASL and JROTC. Western's integration of the ninth-grade counselor and activities around Naviance is another example of integrating PASL with other district priorities.

The importance of integration means that schools wanting to implement PASL should think about their unique assets and existing programs that may serve as points of alignment. The purpose is not to say that some element of PASL is covered because an existing program does it well. Nor is the purpose to completely replace an existing program with PASL's approach to goal achievement. Instead, schools should aim to adapt and integrate PASL's goal-achievement activities into the fabric of the school. Too often, reform initiatives focus on a school's weaknesses. PASL's continuous-improvement approach asks schools to also consider their strengths so that the schools can use them to their advantage and integrate existing initiatives to avoid layering on yet another program.

A final dimension of scale is sustainability.[39] Sustainability, however, does not mean that the reform never changes. Rather, a school's commitment to, and implementation of, the reform with integrity is maintained even as school and district priorities, resources, and other circumstances shift. The shifting priorities in

Broward County Public Schools are evident in the move from a focus on "college and career ready" to "college, career, and life ready." The introduction of Naviance presented another challenge of sustainability because schools had to respond to a districtwide expectation to support students in developing college and career goals. Although the adoption of the personalization period brought opportunities for PASL, it also represented a need to adapt the details of how PASL was implemented. The ability to continuously adapt the implementation practices, while maintaining integrity, also helped further integrate goal achievement into the schools when priorities or other circumstances changed.

These two schools also show how powerful goal achievement can be when it is integrated into a PASL system where the five PASL components reinforce each other. Both schools engaged their educator teams by informing them of the goals that individual students set, and both schools expected multiple people to support the student in progress monitoring. Those goals, and the students' progress toward them, became part of the data system that supported teachers in their work with students. Substantial research demonstrates how school culture shapes students' goal orientation, particularly in high schools.[40] Connecting the school's culture of personalization and learning to developing mastery- or learning-oriented goals and emphasizing the need to continually adjust strategies to achieve goals is critical to the success of goal-achievement interventions.

CHAPTER 5

Component 3: INTENTIONAL USE OF DATA

*Cultivating Multiple Sources of Information
About Students*

Piper High School is located in Sunrise, Florida. Incorporated
in 1961, the city was developed in the 1960s in what were then
the edges of the Everglades. A landlocked city in the center of Broward County, Sunrise experienced high levels of growth through
the 1980s. In these years of suburban expansion, Sunrise was a
destination of new, cutting-edge neighborhoods of ranch houses
and split-level homes. As housing development and the associated
concentration of wealth has shifted west into reclaimed land of
bigger homes in gated communities, the Sunrise neighborhoods
went from being the new, affluent homes to the older, less expen-
sive housing as less-wealthy families moved in. Piper High School,
which opened in 1971, has reflected this shift. In 2016, some 70
percent of students received free and reduced-price lunch. Sixty-
five percent of students identified as Black, 17 percent as Latinx,
and 11 percent as White.

Piper High School serves approximately twenty-four hundred students and has over one hundred teachers. Like many Broward County high schools, it is located in a large, sprawling concrete building. Walking in, a visitor sees a wide hallway that leads to the cafeteria, a large room with high ceilings. The media center is located to the left of the cafeteria, and the school's administration and guidance wing is on the right. Classrooms radiate from this hub. The building is a throwback to the early days of Piper when the school had an "open concept" with no walls between classrooms. Today, the cafeteria is decorated with a giant painting of a Bengal tiger, the school's mascot. The media center is a welcoming and colorful place with college banners lining the walls and posters of prominent Americans encouraging students to read.

As one of the first three schools to implement PASL, Piper's school PASL team tried a couple of approaches in the first two years. During the initial implementation phase, PASL was focused on the entire ninth grade, which constituted approximately 550 ninth-grade students. The following year, the team decided to continue focusing on the ninth grade but to pay particular attention to the ninth graders most at-risk according to their first-quarter academic performance. These targeted students eventually were known as the "Bengal Academy of Excellence," a self-contained group of low performing student who shared the same core teachers. From ten to fifteen teachers were involved; the number fluctuated as teachers moved to other grade levels or retired. The school has always expressed a strong belief in PASL, with Matt Dearen, the PASL coordinator and ninth-grade assistant principal, coining the phrase "PASL to the tassel."

Introducing Data Chats with a Heart

Before PASL, educators at Piper High School had relied on student data to help shape their services to students; the use of data was taken for granted in their daily work. Teachers had been conducting data chats between teachers and students schoolwide for a number of years. With data chats, teachers talked to students about their progress, calling them up to the computer on their desks, drawing from online programs accessible to teachers from the district. For the students in their own classes, teachers turned to Pinnacle, an online grade book, to follow students' progress over the semester. When teachers wanted a broader view across courses and years, they accessed the Virtual Counselor or the Behavioral and Academic Support Information System (BASIS) database, two online repositories of students' grades, attendance, and test scores.

Before it implemented PASL, the school had expected that teachers would conduct data chats twice a quarter—a schedule that had been happening for several years. Teachers always tried to do the chats the week before the interim assessments: four and a half weeks into the nine-week grading period, and then the week before the final grades. They conducted these chats for two reasons. First, academically, the interactions enabled the student to discuss his or her grades and progress with the teacher, talk about assignments that were missing, or explain why the student had been absent. Second, the chats gave that teacher one-on-one time with each student so that the teen could have the teacher's full attention. For Piper teachers, the data chats had been very successful. The adults thought that the chats encouraged students to take more ownership in their education, which was important now that they were at the high school level.

Data chats at Piper received the "PASL touch" in the first year of implementation, when ninth-grade English teachers on the school PASL team realized that they could also use the social-emotional data they were collecting through rapid check-ins and goal-setting achievement in their routine data chats. They noted that the rapid check-in summaries and goal sheets provided information that could help both teachers and students better understand their performance. Teachers said that the original data chats were focused on academics, but that with PASL, the chats naturally led to more social-emotional gateways.

For example, in one of our interviews, a PASL teacher described how he intentionally used the Virtual Counselor database when a student had been frequently absent from his class. The teacher had wondered if the student just didn't like his class. He wondered if she was skipping only his class or if this behavior was more of a trend. By accessing the database, he could look at the student's performance in her other classes to see that she had been missing school, period. At this point, he thought, *How do I take it to the next step and explore this more with the student or their teachers? Their parents?* From the data showing that the student missed more than just his class, he considered whether the student's lack of attendance might be caused by an issue at home. On further discussion with her, he learned she had stopped coming to school because she had to go to her job. Her mom was very sick, and it was either pay the bills or be evicted. This information helped the teacher understand the student and make sure that other adults also understood the situation and would try to work with her so that she could continue coming to school.

At Piper, these kinds of data chats that bridged academic data with information about students' social-emotional activities came to be called *Data Chats with a Heart*. The "heart" part of the data chat came from how the teacher interacted with the student around the data. Before the introduction of PASL, the teachers had seen the data chats as a required check-in with a student about grades. With PASL and the additional information from rapid check-ins and goal-achievement lessons, the teachers were reminded about their importance as a source of support for the student. Instead of seeing the interaction as a transaction, they sought to build a relationship with each student.

In another example, another PASL teacher shared that when having Data Chats with a Heart with failing students, she would tell them about the first and only F she received in her life. It happened in high school in one of her favorite subjects, English. "I give them my own life stories," she said. "I say, 'I think I lived this so that I can help you.'" Data Chats with a Heart were also described by adults as a way of documentation for both the teacher and the student, a way for both of them to get on the same page regarding the teacher's expectations and the student's motivation.

Administrators and teachers said that Data Chats with a Heart helped students take ownership of their learning experiences in a more holistic way. Dearen explained it this way: "It's a way of documentation for the teacher and the student—of where they're going with their average, what they're missing. You know, documentation that goes from school to home and then back, you know, as far as, 'Hey, we said this, we had a chat about this, if you'd like to come in and meet with all the teachers, here's, you know, the arrangements.' But definitely, data chats help the students take ownership."

For low performing students, the chats were particularly powerful and enabled the student to be understood and seen. At Piper High School, the teachers had data chats more frequently with the students they identified as the highest risk. Another unique feature of Piper was the presence of a behavior specialist at the school. PASL teachers could talk about their struggling students with this professional, Stephane Monereau, who would then offer additional ongoing support to monitor the students. With the data that teachers shared with the specialist in the form of attendance reports and grades, he would then connect with the students themselves to conduct his own Data Chats with a Heart to learn more about the underlying issues. Some teachers did voice concerns that they would learn too many details of students' personal lives or were not comfortable sharing too many details of their own lives. The same was true for some students, who also reported that they were also not used to teachers opening up to them in such ways. Generally, though, there was a consensus that data chats were helpful. As one student explained, a teacher "helped me push back and get my grade up, but so after I had, like, a C, I think I went back up to a low A or a high B."

Exposing the heart within this existing practice was an essential component of PASL. Data Chats with a Heart were not just about a teacher's conversation with a student about academics. The conversations could also be an act of caring. Additional information could also help round out the teachers' understanding of a student so that the adult and the student could connect on more than just one level. Not only did this outcome hold for teachers, but it also went all the way to the principal, as we will discuss shortly.

A Data-Rich Environment

American high schools are awash with student performance data, and Florida public schools have been at the forefront of this data use. At the state level, Florida was an early adopter of test-based accountability. As a result, Florida public schools have a strong culture of using student test scores and other data to identify and track student progress. School administrators, guidance counselors, and teachers have access to information on students' attendance, course grades, disciplinary infractions, scores on state assessments, and other data over multiple years if the student has stayed in the district. Florida districts have built their own data systems that give their staff access to interim assessment grades and progress monitoring indicators. Gone are the days when a student entered a classroom as a blank slate; now teachers have the option to review their students' academic performance, attendance, and history of disciplinary infractions before the children enter the classroom in the fall. Florida policies such as the A+ policy, which grades schools according to performance measures, student promotion policies, and teacher merit pay, all reinforce the reliance and management of data in districts and schools across the state.

Like many other districts in Florida, Broward County Public Schools began building a robust data infrastructure through its data warehouse in the mid-1990s. In addition to having a longitudinal database with multiple student and teacher indicators, the district provided different tools with different purposes. Through the data warehouse and the district's Office of School Climate and Discipline, the district developed BASIS, which it describes as "the comprehensive District electronic tool providing *all* the data needed to drive decision-making and instruction in schools."[1] When accessing BASIS, Broward educators not only had access to individual students' data profile, but also saw a green, yellow, or red light, indicating to the viewer whether the student was in danger of failing his or her grade. Through the warehouse, the district also developed Virtual Counselor. Whereas BASIS is accessible only to Broward County Public Schools staff, Virtual Counselor gave parents and students access to similar year-by-year data. The district also built Pinnacle, the online grade book where students, parents, and teachers can access students' progress through their coursework. In an effort to monitor student progress during the No Child Left Behind (NCLB) years, the district also administered quarterly interim assessments of the students' progress in language arts and mathematics over an academic year, before the state's spring assessments. The district stopped administering these in 2013, when the state received a waiver regarding participation in NCLB.

During our year-long research in four Broward County high schools in 2010–2011, we found that the schools worked in a data-rich environment and that the adults there drew on data to inform both administrative and instructional practices. At that time, adults at three of the four schools favorably viewed the use of data, saying that it allowed them, for example, to identify students who were receiving Fs in class and to provide them with support.[2] We found that "the administrators, guidance counselors, and teachers at the higher performing schools were more likely to describe using data for personalization and culture building and not just as an instrumental tool for goal setting and monitoring."[3] During the design phase of the district PASL team activities (fall 2012), we found that the adults saw data as a tool that facilitated decision-making in their work and that supported both themselves and the students.

In the initial design phase, as the district PASL team worked to turn the research findings into an implementable and scalable reform, we were not surprised that the systemic use of data emerged as a stand-alone core component of personalization efforts. District and school members of the team were already viewing the use of student data as an essential feature of their work. These records informed curricular, instructional, guidance, and administrative decisions. The design team members advocated for making data use a central feature of the PASL model because they saw data as a powerful tool supporting their work with students and teachers.

While the team was advocating for having data as a stand-alone component, it was also using data to inform the design and reform process. In the design phase, as discussed earlier in the book, the district PASL team used data to guide its model. The three pilot schools delved into their school-level and student-level data to better understand the attitudes and needs of adults and students at their school. They also generated their own data, through surveys and focus groups of students and adults. As the PASL work moved into the implementation phase and we began the PDSA cycles, improvement data took center stage as schools studied their PASL processes. Data, therefore, played a central role in PASL as a core component of the model and as a tool for personalization and improvement.

Data as a Tool of Personalization

By including the intentional use of data as a component of PASL, the district PASL team members were building on a culture of data use already present in their schools and district. Indeed, studies have found that reform efforts are more successful if schools expand and strengthen practices and programs already present at their school site.[4] In the context of data use, the members drew on data generated at the district level and the school level to support their practices, but they also relied on structures in which they were generating and building data use on a local level. By including the intentional use of data as part of the PASL model, they were not only continuing and building on current practices, but also building on their experience of using data to inform the personalization process.

How can student data be used as a tool for personalization? PASL team members recognized that different kinds of data provide information about students' individual academic and social-emotional experiences in schools. Rapid check-ins, goal-achievement activities, and educator teams count on, and are enriched with, in-depth information. Research has similarly shown that student achievement data can be leveraged for instructional improvement.[5] Information about students is enhanced when adults draw from data demonstrating students' behavioral and social-emotional skill levels. [6] Grades are understood in the research not only as information about students' academic progress, but also for reflecting social-emotional elements such as student behavior, participation, and effort.[7]

In addition to providing information about individual students, data systems allow schools to generate and aggregate information about the whole school or subsets of students. Schools use this aggregated data to improve personalization with students and subgroups of students, uncovering trends that can help identify problems and areas of improvement, such as ninth-grade attendance or eleventh and twelfth graders' readiness to graduate. Administrators also use data as a tool to build school culture and to inform their administrative decisions. Data can, for example, be used to assign students to teachers, if a teacher shows demonstrated successes with a particular population of students, or to figure out if the school needs to direct extra resources in reading or math.[8] By looking at whole-school or subgroup trends, adults in schools make important choices about how to dispense and use resources.

Research on Data Practices

Research on how educators use data is not usually cast in terms of facilitating personalization. Arguably, personalization is one of data's major uses; the data provides a perspective into student progress that influences the type of support and services given to all students, both individually and as a collective. When used well, information about students provides personal knowledge that can help teachers, administrators, support staff, and the students themselves make effective decisions. For this reason, district PASL team members conceived of using data both to provide insight into individual students and to connect the other components of PASL.[9]

As computer data systems have become more common in districts and schools, educators have hailed them as a tool to support decision-making for individual students and for school-level decisions such as hiring, course assignment, and teacher evaluations.[10] Part of a teacher's daily routine is to make classroom decisions, many of which are based on their own data collected by informal observations and formative assessments of students. When teachers use data for instructional purposes, they identify and diagnose student performance to modify instruction or to provide extra academic support for students.[11]

Data also becomes a tool for teachers to use with colleagues in their professional development. Studies find that when teachers work in teams, they draw on multiple forms of data to enrich their conversations about improving classroom practices, services to students, and school programs and policies. Whether data is used in professional learning communities, department meetings, or simple discussions about groups of students, the information offers a powerful tool to share solutions, leading to greater organizational coherence.[12]

However, studies have found that teachers' capacity for using data effectively can vary with training and local conditions. As Julie Marsh and Caitlin Farrell explain, teachers do not always know how to employ data to further their curricular and instructional practices and may "lack adequate skills and knowledge to formulate questions, select indicators, and identify solutions."[13] They emphasize that it is important to help teachers have the skills to use data effectively. Studies also find that school conditions need to facilitate the teams' use of data to support effective communication, professional development that helps users obtain the required knowledge and skills, and leadership that facilitates data use.[14] These studies emphasize the importance of a culture of data use where adults in schools feel supported and valued as they use data to guide and solve educational issues.

School leaders also play an important role in developing teacher capacity to make data-driven decisions.[15] The leaders set the culture of how data will be used. They provide an infrastructure that facilitates adults' capabilities in data use, either individually or collectively.[16] They draw from aggregated data to adapt their school-level policies, such as where to direct resources, while remaining true to the school's vision and mission. School leaders play a critical role in setting data routines and culture.

While some data systems in school provide insight into students' academic, behavioral, and social-emotional progress, the adults also build and draw on their own data as part of continuous improvement. Data can be a tool to facilitate organizational learning and to target specific goals. Each cycle of data use for continuous improvement involves several sequential steps: (1) data capture, (2) interpretation, (3) information sharing, and (4) knowledge organization.[17] To gather data, schools employ other strategies, such as focus groups, surveys, analyses of student work, and assessments of students' extracurricular activities, to complement the formal data provided by the district. Together, these practices contribute to structured reflection and improvement.

Whether data is used as a tool for understanding a student's academic progress, as a resource for teachers in problem-solving, as a way for leaders to shape their organizational goals, or as a vehicle to support continuous improvement, the intentional use of data provides valuable information to stakeholders. The ultimate goal of data use is to improve resources for students.

Two More PASL Schools Use Data

As schools began to implement PASL, they used data in various ways. Sometimes they drew from Pinnacle, the online grade book, to follow up on a rapid check-in to see if a student's grade had fluctuated in the course. Other times teachers, guidance counselors, and administrators turned to BASIS, the district's resource for student data, to discuss students receiving Ds and Fs on their interim report cards. Other times schools generated their own data, such as information from the rapid check-ins or from students' goal-sharing activities. Or the school might have a shared file, where adults could see comments on each student.

As discussed earlier, several district-designed computer programs already in place in many of the district's schools were compatible with the goals of PASL. The presence of these programs was not surprising, given the district's long commitment to data and related data systems. When introduced to the intentional use of data as a feature of PASL, many teachers questioned how this feature was different from what "good teachers" already did with their students and data. This perspective was somewhat common until they learned more about using data intentionally and how it bridged components of PASL, such as with Data Chats with a Heart. Once school leaders and teachers realized how this practice helped complement the other PASL components, they began to understand that intentionally using data as part of the system of PASL was different from isolated uses of data.

At-a-Glance Reports at Piper High School

Another resource Piper teachers found particularly helpful for summarizing the academic data was something called *at-a-glance reports*, which were provided by the school administration. Teachers described these reports as a breakdown of student performance during the previous four weeks, timed just after each interim grade report and report cards. The first part included information about the demographics of each grade level, including the numbers of all students, Exceptional Student Education students, and English Language Learners students and other general information. Most of the time, total student numbers ranged between five hundred and seven hundred per grade level. Then the report listed the students who would be taking different statewide assessment tests.

It also listed attendance, including a list of students who had ten or more absences.

Teachers told us that the at-a-glance reports assisted them in identifying who needed special education services through the response-to-intervention (RTI) process—"because this report is able to give us a snapshot of what cohorts of students we're dealing with." RTI had only started at Piper two years before PASL was introduced, and teachers reported that PASL was compatible with the expectations of RTI. An administrator explained it this way:

> [RTI is] really difficult for high schools, because of the time aspect, because in a perfect world, you want to be able to sit with that team at least once or twice a month to look at these lists of students. All right, so you've got your overage students, you've got your students with attendance issues, you've got your students with Fs. Our school psychologist has more than one school, so they're only here once a week. Then we have our guidance counselors and our directors. They're dealing with students throughout the day—right now, they're dealing with course selection cards, where they've got to see every single class. So at the beginning of the year, they're dealing with registrations, where they've got to put all the information into the system. Then they're seeing students individually. Then they're dealing with parent conferences. I mean, it's a lot, man.

The administrator went on to explain that the at-a-glance reports provided valuable data to build on. For all the adults in the school, the reports set common expectations of the students' characteristics and needs.

Data Teaming, Teacher to Teacher

As discussed earlier, we found that many of the schools had PASL-like structures before we began the implementation, but educators realized that PASL built on and strengthened these existing practices. For example, Piper High School focused on *data teaming*, the practice of teachers meeting with one another to discuss struggling students. Schools followed this practice in different ways, but at Piper, teachers gave the example of their US history classes. All these classes would take a test on the Cold War. Once they had the results, the teachers would grade them and then look at the scores together. They would jointly discuss topics such as questions most frequently missed and the terminology the students were lacking. Then they would discuss how they could reteach the topic. Or if people were doing well in the subject, they would consider how they could offer enrichment incentives.

The teachers conducted data teaming across content areas such as science and English every Tuesday from 7:15 to 7:30 a.m., on what the teachers called Academic Tuesdays. One teacher described these meetings as a quick, very meat-and-potatoes meeting where "people bring their data. It's not really coffee talk. It's like, 'Hey, here's what we're doing, here's where my students are at. What about you?'" With only fifteen minutes, teachers, not surprisingly, felt pressured by the limited time. But they used this time as effectively as they could and considered it worthwhile.

A Principal's Perspective: Information Both for Students and for Teachers

Piper's principal, Angel Gomez, emphasized the importance of the data and reports: "It's not about just making those reports look pretty. It's about those reports having substance." The "substance" that he referred to related to how data can tell a principal that a program is working. Specifically, Gomez's interest centered on knowing how PASL was working (or not) in his school and to what extent the data influenced that effectiveness. Of greatest interest was student outcome data. Early on, for example, Gomez looked at the rates of ninth-grade suspensions from one year to the next, in the first quarter. He said that he clearly remembered the data about the number of suspensions:

> It was dramatically low, and I don't know if PASL is the reason why. I mean, there's so many variables. We're talking about a different class of students, you know. It's a different group of kids, so I'm not comparing kids to kids, okay? I could follow the cohort, right, but those have also gone down. But PASL is definitely something that adds to that positive change, no question about it. It actually brings a level of awareness not just for the student but also for the teacher. Then the teacher is able to see a little more beyond certain things. Before, they could not get past those [suspensions], and now they see them not as an attack to them personally, but as a sign of something that the kid may need help with something, okay? So it's helping the teachers . . .
>
> We have one thing that we can offer, and that's a high school diploma. And we're going to do everything we can to make sure that you get it and that you can do anything that you want with it. And that's the college- and career-readiness piece.

He emphasized that the data chat was a piece of documentation for the *student*. Teachers could print out a report for each of their students to show where the student was at any point, and they used that piece for academic matters. But it did not stop there. PASL brought a name and a more intentional and systematic way to use the information that many teachers were already gathering in their data chats. Once adapted, PASL gave educators at Piper High School a way to organize the academic and social-emotional information about their students into a simpler framework that was much easier to use purposefully with their colleagues, the parents, but especially with their students.

Building Data Resources: Adaptation and Spread

Like other schools in Florida, Broward County high schools had strong cultures of data use. Perhaps not surprisingly, then, other schools implementing PASL considered the use of data as essential to their schools. We now turn to two scale-out schools' intentional approaches to using data.

WESTERN HIGH SCHOOL: THE PASL TAB

As PASL began to expand beyond the three pilot schools, schools continued to use data as a core component of their reform efforts. The scaling of PASL to new schools also brought challenges to the infrastructure that was supporting the use of data for personalization and continuous improvement. At Western High School, principal Jimmy Arrojo's vision was for all students to feel as if they had a place where they could grow and reach their full potential without fear and where people would treat them with dignity and respect. To build this inclusive environment in one of the largest high schools in the county, the school's PASL team members needed a way to share information about students with each other.

As the PASL coordinator and ninth-grade assistant principal, Derek Gordon worked at the front lines to generate ninth-grade data for the other educators in the building. Like other schools, the school already had, by the 2015–2016 school year, the habit of tracking all its students. But Gordon realized that by adding a shared file accessible to all ninth-grade teachers, the staff could track rapid check-ins and goal-achievement lessons with students as well. Gordon tailored a FileMaker Pro file and gave all the ninth-grade teachers access. In the shared file, all the students were listed, and the teachers noted rapid check-ins, students' goals, and any challenges they had discovered in their interactions with students. To keep a running record, the teachers documented in the system the date they talked to the students. There was also a place where they could type in notes, such as a comment that a student was trying out for volleyball or was looking for a tutor.

Gordon continued to provide D/F reports to teachers, documenting the students with low grades, as was common throughout the district. The teachers told the school PASL team, however, that they did not have the time to search through the reports to find their own students. In response, Gordon began disaggregating the D/F report information for each teacher, providing the list at weeks four and nine of each quarter. He would also download the students' goals from Naviance, pull them into an Excel spreadsheet, and then add the spreadsheet to the FileMaker Pro file. In turn, teachers used this information to initiate a conversation with a student or to talk about something going on in class.

The result was very useful to teachers for their PASL activities but time-consuming for Gordon. As a member of the original district PASL team, Gordon was in a strong leadership position to build capacity around data not only at Western but also district-wide. At the quarterly network meetings, Gordon met with our full team and, more importantly, with other school teams and the district leaders. From discussions with these stakeholders and feedback from his own school team, he took the lead in building a resource in the district BASIS online tool. Called the *PASL tab*, it was a section with data only about PASL students. His goal was to replicate the platform he had created in FileMaker Pro in a way that was less time-intensive at the school level. He worked closely with John Tienjaroonkui, a teacher from Flanagan High School, another original pilot school, to share the PASL tab idea with the district's Office of Information and Technology. The office was receptive to the idea.

In the summer of 2017, Tienjaroonkui worked with the district to develop a mock-up of the PASL tab. The desired data included lists of the students with five or more absences, students with GPAs below 2.0 at the end of every semester, students with one or more referrals, and, at the request of one of the high school directors, the number of students with Fs in English, math, and science. Just like the FileMaker Pro file that educators at Western had used to share data, the PASL tab allowed administrators, guidance counselors, and teachers to identify their PASL students; search for their own students; and see academic, PASL, and other data. Administrators and guidance counselors could also make their own groups in the system, such as students who had three or more failures. The PASL tab in BASIS further institutionalized the reform as a district process, sending signals about the importance of multiple indicators of student progress and success.

POMPANO BEACH HIGH SCHOOL: A VORTEX OF INFORMATION

Pompano Beach High School, introduced earlier in the book, offers another window into how schools make effective use of data. As a magnet school open to high performing students across the district, Pompano Beach became interested in implementing PASL to address student retention. The school required its students to maintain a 2.5 GPA to remain enrolled, but some students faced challenges with meeting this expectation. Before the implementation of PASL, some ten to twelve students left the ninth grade each year. The school PASL team had received feedback that the school's strong focus on academics had been difficult for some students who were already coming from long distances to attend the school.

Concerned about student apathy, lack of academic focus, and entitlement, the team members sought to use PASL as a way to build connections with students, help them feel a stronger sense of belonging, and sustain their past academic successes. As the members learned more about Western's use of FileMaker Pro, they realized that this platform would be a useful tool for them as well.

They decided to call it Vortex, a riff on the school's nickname, the Golden Tornados. Both the assistant principal, Jill Samaroo, and the ninth-grade guidance counselor, Lori Carlson, had access to teachers' participation in the document. Ideally, every two weeks, teachers were expected to record their rapid check-ins in this system and input in the comment box any additional information that might be of interest to the broader team. As at Western, the PASL coordinator/ninth-grade administrator and the PASL teachers all had access to this file, which, like Western's file, included rapid check-in information.

The guidance counselor regularly tracked students identified as having problems, paying particular attention to the students' GPAs. In 2016, Carlson explained: "I think the PASL program is giving us that opportunity to really look at kids. Not that we didn't look at kids before, but I think it's more conscious and intentional . . . and maybe it's more in ninth grade because we do look at a fragile time with that transition. How do you get from middle school to high school, find independence, and exert yourself as your own learner and make decisions, knowing sometimes you don't always make the best ones when you're fourteen or fifteen?"

With students whose files showed that they were struggling, Carlson would call them into her office to talk about grades and to see if other resources would be helpful. She would sometimes follow up with parents as well. Pompano Beach continued to use Vortex and to add information the school deemed relevant to students—information such as extracurricular activities or their peer mentor. Carlson told us that the school had fewer and fewer students leaving, something it credited to PASL. Over the years, the school also sought to put more responsibility for the GPAs in the hands of students (see chapter 7). The school's use of Vortex helped institutionalize PASL into the lives of educators and students.

Conclusion

Broward County high schools were already drawing on student data before 2010. Our original study of Broward County Public Schools identified data use as an effective practice.[18] Not surprisingly, then, the district PASL team members advocated it as a stand-alone component of PASL. In this chapter, we have shown how schools tailored the intentional use of data to their own school situations, building on prior practices, learning strategies from new schools, and institutionalizing routines over time both at the school and within the district's online databases. Translating rapid check-ins and goal achievement into shareable data helped provide information about PASL students to other educators. Data use in education is ultimately about providing information to educators, students, and parents to assist with student progress. When the data is linked to interactions and discussions with students, it helps adults make the connection between numbers on a screen and the real person at their desk, responding to their hellos.

CHAPTER 6

Component 4: EDUCATOR TEAMS

Collaborative Problem Solving with Colleagues

Educator teams have been a central feature of the PASL model since its collaborative design and development (chapter 2). These teams bring teachers, guidance counselors, and administrators together as part of the system of PASL. They share information gained about students through the other components of rapid check-ins, goal-achievement lessons, and the intentional use of data. With purposeful conversations about students and personalization, the adults in schools build relationships with their peers, share their experiences with students, build community, and consequently contribute to the culture of personalization at their school. Like all the components of PASL, school teams have the discretion to establish the extent, size, and composition of their educator teams. In so doing, they consider the needs of students, teachers, and the school generally. In this chapter, we discuss the role and potential of educator teams to build school community.

To understand the potential of educator teams, we again begin with the story of Blanche Ely High School. Earlier in this book, we discussed how the school team at Ely, led by PASL coordinator/ninth-grade assistant principal Cherie Hodgson-Toeller, had developed Cross-Talks, a collaborative approach to educator teams. During their Cross-Talks, which were scheduled during quarterly professional-development time, teachers identified one student in their Power of Period One class who was struggling on the D/F lists. They discussed this student with another teacher who also had this student. Beginning in the second year of its implementation of PASL, Ely had added regular meetings among the ninth-grade teachers through a dedicated professional learning community. To build community, the teachers who were the first adopters of PASL became ambassadors who could mentor teachers beginning to participate in the PASL learning community. Ely High School, therefore, followed three practices that brought teachers together as educator teams: the Cross-Talks, the ninth-grade teacher team, and the PASL ambassadors.

In our conversations with teachers at Ely, we heard that collaboration among teachers had not always been easy. A group of teachers had attended Ely as high schoolers, lived in the community, and felt a strong sense of connection to the school. It had been difficult for them to connect with newer teachers, many of whom had rotated in and out of the school over the years because of high teacher turnover. With their concern for student attendance, discipline, grades, and student scores on the state assessment, teachers at Ely described a demanding school environment, one that did not engender strong collegiality. Yet teachers had very positive feedback on Cross-Talks and the ninth-grade teacher team. The school PASL team also recognized its role in adapting PASL at Ely. Together, when the teachers met as a group, the interaction helped build a common feeling of purpose. It also helped teachers get to know each other better.

Teachers recognized that Cross-Talks were a helpful way to build knowledge around a struggling student. They said that the meetings not only helped the students but also increased collaboration between teachers. Administrators also recognized that Cross-Talks helped identify students in need of extra attention. As one explained,

> So we had not only the one Power of Period One teacher, but now we had a partner in crime, if you will, meeting with them to discuss: 'What strategies have you done? What strategies have I done? You know, let's try this for the next nine weeks and kinda see how that's working out, report back, and track it.' And then we took it to a larger level and we had what we call large Cross-Talk focus groups, where teachers could say then, 'This is what I've been doing with my focus student, this is what's working, this isn't what's working, this is how we need administration to help us, this is where we're struggling, this is what we're seeing, these are the gains we've had, but here's still where we have problems, attendance,' or whatever it happens to be.

During the twenty- to thirty-minute block of time, the teachers discussed their identified student and the strategies that they used with him or her. Often, a teacher discovered that a student was performing better with the other teacher, and the first teacher learned strategies that would help. Ninth-grade teachers, who met monthly, found that this approach helped them have a more holistic view of the students in their classes. They also said it helped them get to know their colleagues better as well.

At the end of each nine weeks, the school would also have schoolwide Cross-Talks, which engaged teachers beyond the ninth grade. The adults appreciated that this time was built into the already-planned professional-development days, unlike other schools, whose PASL teams met before or after school.

Having a professional learning community created a space for the ninth-grade teachers to discuss PASL issues and plan PASL activities such as their goal-achievement lessons. The teachers explained that because they often felt isolated, the monthly professional learning communities allowed them to share their experiences at Ely with other teachers. The teachers also described coming to the meeting ready to talk about the success of goal-achievement lessons or their frustration with the support provided to students. They believed that they received important information and support at these meetings. They also described how they bounced ideas off each other and how the meetings were a place where they could problem-solve. As one teacher explained, "I think the teachers . . . use the Power of Period One to identify issues. And they use Cross-Talk to collaborate on issues. And after trying their own strategies for interventions, if those don't work, then they refer those to the team." If the teachers had a good idea that worked and was related to PASL activities, the learning community was the forum where they could freely share it.

This strategy particularly resonated with teachers new to the school and who appreciated being included as part of the PASL learning community. They explained that the intentional nature of PASL provided them with a shared topic of conversation from the first week of school and helped them feel immediately part of a community. It was also useful when new teachers came on board later in the school year and did not get the opportunity to receive the professional development about PASL offered at the initial planning. One new teacher called this meeting her "lifeline." Teachers got to know each other during the PASL learning community, but also saw it as an opportunity to learn more about the Ely culture. One teacher called this a "welcome to Ely" kind of session.

The PASL learning community was also a helpful resource for teachers who were sometimes not as confident in conducting PASL activities right away. Some teachers confessed they weren't sure if they were "doing it right" or understanding PASL correctly at first. For instance, they wondered if they were supposed to do rapid check-ins once a week, once a day, or on some other schedule. Teachers would casually speak to teachers who were more familiar with PASL, but the less experienced teachers had mixed feelings about the helpfulness of these interactions. They realized they needed to reach out to different resources, and the PASL learning community gave them a space to do so. The community also made new teachers feel as if they belonged to something. This sense of belonging is particularly important because of how easy it is for teachers to retreat to their classroom, do their job, and then leave. New teachers at Ely High School always felt that they had support, whereas teachers at other schools did not feel the same way.

In the second year of their participation, the PASL leadership at Ely decided to have the experienced teachers serve as PASL ambassadors to either the new teachers or the teachers new to PASL. As one teacher explained, "Since last year, we had a group of ten teachers who were doing [PASL]. We were teaching it; they were teaching it to us. And then this year, we are the ambassadors of PASL. So, we're passing it to the other teachers where we have teachers that we work with." This structure helped the more experienced teachers become the experts, sharing their experiences with the newly adopting teachers.

As a group, the teachers and other administrators thought that both Cross-Talks and the PLC were places where they could share ideas with other faculty and staff. At a large school where people sometimes felt isolated, these interactions gave them a clear space to share ideas and discuss students. The PASL ambassadors helped

legitimize and spread the norms and expectations of personalization to new teachers. For teachers who had felt isolated, this
structured time to collaborate and share with peers helped build
a welcoming community.[1]

Research on Educator Teams

Like many of the other component of PASL, educator teams represent an organizational strategy already present in high schools.
To be sure, teacher routinely collaborate in schools. Effective
schools have been described as team-based organizations where
adults come together to talk about a specific objective, mandate,
or policy in the service of students.[2] Educator teams can take
many forms. Teachers collaborate with others who are in the same
student grade and who teach the same subject matter. There are
formal collaborations based on PLCs and informal ones where, for
example, teachers eat lunch or share a hallway. Teachers may participate on their principal's leadership team. They may take roles as
curriculum developers. Although high schools have been described
as balkanized, with their structure based on subject-matter departments much like silos, we see many formal and informal examples
of educator teams in high schools.[3]

Across K–12 education, studies have found that high-quality
teacher collaboration is associated with higher student achievement. Schools with stronger collaborative environments have
higher student achievement gains.[4] While teacher evaluation systems often assume that teachers are independent of each other,
research has shown that collaboration means that one teacher's
instruction is improved when the person works in teams with more
effective peers.[5] High-quality teacher collaboration is a powerful
practice that helps teachers build relationships and improve their
work with their students.

Many formal educator-team structures are already quite familiar to educators. Small learning communities have been at the core of school reform efforts to personalize schools for over a decade. Whether the communities are labeled *schools within schools, small schools, houses,* or *teams,* the basic premise is to develop collaborative communities within schools as a central strategy for improving student learning. Scholars posit that the central focus across the creation of small learning communities is to "create 'conditions' that engage students, support leaning, and enhance development."[6] A growing body of evidence supports the idea that small learning communities can improve student achievement, performance, and adjustment in middle school and high school.[7] Evidence also suggests that the personalized environments created in these communities, when fully implemented, consistently have even larger effects on social-emotional and academic outcomes for students from socially and economically disadvantaged backgrounds (e.g., students of color or economically disadvantaged students).

Professional learning communities are another familiar and promising form of educator teams that facilitate learning for both students and teachers. Studies find that when implemented well, these communities help change teacher cultures toward greater collaboration, an increased focus on student learning, greater teacher authority, and stronger cycles of teacher learning.[8] Education professor Vicki Vescio and colleagues explain that these learning communities "shift teachers' habits of mind and create cultures of teaching that engage educators in enhancing teacher and student learning."[9]

This is not to say educator collaboration does not occur in other high school settings; it just tends to happen a little differently. A more robust research base on educator collaboration exists for the elementary level, mainly because high school departments have difficulty finding common times to meet—challenges elementary school teams with common schedules are not faced with as frequently.[10] Studies do find that when teachers meet within their subject-matter communities, they gain important collective knowledge about their disciplines.[11]

When viewed with the lens of PASL, educator teams must be understood as ways for teachers to come together to talk intentionally about student needs and ways to enhance the student experience. Along the way, teachers establish a greater sense of connection to the school and to their colleagues.

We identify three elements required in PASL educator teams. First, the teams must include all the teachers who are implementing PASL so that all these adults are collaborating professionally. Second, the school must set aside time for PASL teachers to meet and engage meaningfully around students and PASL activities. This practice not only signals that the school values these conversations, but also provides educators the time to share experiences and address problems. Third, when PASL educator teams meet, the teachers must have the autonomy to identify their areas of focus and what they believe best serves their PASL goals. They must be supported by administrators and guidance counselors, but they must also be granted the space to decide on the best path forward for students.

Creating New Educator Teams in Broward County Public Schools

Among Broward County Public Schools, each school was responsible for identifying how it would create its PASL educator teams. The idea was that routine meetings between teachers and other adults in the school to discuss students would help direct important resources to students in need. These meetings would also provide teachers with a community to share important information, to receive support generally, and, finally, to discuss PASL.

PASL educator teams brought together high school administrators—usually an assistant principal—guidance counselors, and grade-level PASL teachers who shared a subset of PASL students. Each of these teachers was responsible for conferring with these students through rapid check-ins. In turn, this rapid check-in data was then compiled with other social-emotional data (e.g., goals), academic data (e.g., grades), and administrative data (e.g., attendance) as the team engaged in more intentional uses of the data at the meetings. These various data sources revealed the holistic needs of the PASL students, and the educator team could then discuss these needs and address them with a better base of evidence.

Originally, the district PASL team had envisioned both an educator team and a core team, the latter consisting of an assistant principal, a guidance counselor, and lead teachers. The district PASL team thought that the core team would be responsible for planning the PASL program activities and meeting with identified students to solve problems. The district team had also expected the core team to loop with its cohort of students. Looping has proved to be an effective process that decreases student anxiety, increases student achievement, supports instructional time, and provides sustained relationships between adults in the school and students and parents.[12] In most schools that we worked with, the responsibilities of this core team either dissolved into the sole purview of the assistant principal (who, in almost all schools, served as the PASL school coordinator) or the educator teams. We believe that the core team dissolved mostly because of teachers' time constraints and because the assistant principal's role was already aligned with these same responsibilities.

We now turn to two other Broward County schools that organized educator teams. Along with the earlier example of Ely, these schools offer different perspectives of how educator teams were adapted to different school environments while still maintaining the integrity of the innovation. Western High School, as one of the scale-out schools, learned from Blanche Ely High School and adapted the idea of Cross-Talks to fit its own school situation in the form of Wildcat Chats. At Pompano Beach High School, the educators took an intentional approach to the educator team's composition and, like Ely High School, adapted the team to their own school's unique circumstances.

WESTERN HIGH SCHOOL: A PROFESSIONAL LEARNING COMMUNITY TO PLAN WILDCAT CHATS

Western High School joined PASL in the second year of implementation. It also had a PASL professional learning community (PLC), originally consisting of seven ninth-grade teachers and the guidance counselor, led by a school coordinator. When these seven teachers started, they had just under two hundred students and later became the school's leadership team for PASL. By 2018–2019 there were approximately thirty-two teachers, each of whom worked with a focal group of twenty-five ninth-grade students, who together constituted the entire ninth grade. Every semester, the core leadership team of teachers received a temporary duty authorization, a day off from teaching, where they could come together and plan. During this time, they created the lesson plans that were run through the personalization periods, and they organized Wildcat Chats, their school's version of Cross-Talks, which they adapted to for their school's needs. In Western's first year of PASL reform, the activities were mainly conducted in fourth-period classes. But once the district's newly formed personalization period was established, PASL activities took place during this study hall, which the schools and teachers could decide to use for PASL purposes.

The PASL teachers at Western organized Wildcat Chats slightly differently than did the Ely teachers. Each Western teacher nominated a student that he or she believed would benefit from a discussion with the rest of the teachers. Unlike at Ely, where the teachers focused on the students receiving Ds or Fs, the teachers focused on the students that were doing well in most of their classes but were maybe struggling in one or two. Teachers across departments would come together about strategies that were working in the classes where the students were doing well, and the adults implemented these strategies in the classes where the students were having trouble. The teachers also set goals, shared best practices, and tested different strategies.

By 2017–2018, the PASL team teachers met more routinely as a PLC every two weeks, for a half hour in the morning, before classes started. Additional time was provided quarterly through temporary duty authorizations. As discussed throughout this book, PASL continues to adapt at Western High School. The school has undeniably benefited from strong leadership from assistant principal Derek Gordon and the principal, Jimmy Arrojo. However, others have also embraced personalization as an important way to build the school community.

POMPANO BEACH HIGH SCHOOL: DISTRIBUTED TEAMS, COMMON TIME

Pompano Beach High School is located near Blanche Ely and was initially a satellite campus. In the first year of the school's implementation of PASL, all ninth graders participated in PASL activities, which occurred during their first period, similar to Ely. When the district added the personalization period, Pompano Beach changed how it assigned students to their PASL teacher. During the ninth graders' orientation, all of them were paired with one of their core subject teachers, who also became their PASL teacher and met with them in the personalization period.

Pompano Beach's experience illustrates the perplexing question "When will we have time to meet?," a question that schools often face. Unlike the teams at other PASL schools, the core educator team at Pompano Beach was composed of representatives from each of the departments. This variety afforded the team with a distributed level of expertise among the content-area teachers. Having this structure of a smaller core team rather than a larger team of all the participating teachers also made it easier to find a common time to meet. These teachers then acted as mentors to the other small groups of participating PASL teachers in their respective departments, which already had existing times to meet as a department. Through this collaboration, teachers tailored their PASL activities to themes that were already being covered in the content areas. For example, English teachers conducted a lesson on decision-making in English class when they were covering *Romeo and Juliet*. Additionally, the mentors were available for any questions about how to conduct rapid check-ins, which lesson plans they should be implementing, gathering the lesson plans for their month, and helping their teachers to implement them.

At the beginning of the year and during teacher planning, the core team conducted training for all the PASL teachers and did a gallery walk of posters to explain what the reform was all about. The posters shared the goals of PASL and explained its different components. The members of the core educator team stood at each of the posters, so that it was not the administrators who were explaining PASL to the teachers. The PASL coordinator thought that the information had to come from the teachers who really believed in each of the components. "It wasn't from the top down," the coordinator said. "It was from the teachers' mouths to theirs."

The educator team at Pompano Beach found it particularly difficult to arrange a common time to meet. Part of the challenge was attributed to how academically focused the teachers were; they simply did not want to be out of class. Initially, the educator team met about once a quarter, in addition to the meetings that convened the PASL teams from all schools. The PASL coordinator would rotate the teacher to attend these day-long meetings with PASL team members from other schools.

During the spring of the first year, administrators provided the PASL team with substitute teachers for a half day so that the team members could meet to discuss their shared students. To accomplish this logistically, the school hired approximately ten substitutes for the day and released ten teachers in the morning and then teachers in the afternoon. Then the next day, the school followed this same routine, with five additional teachers in the morning. In the afternoon, the core team was provided free time to debrief and make plans for the next year.

Many issues emerged during this half-day meeting. The teachers had many concerns (e.g., "huge attendance issues") that they had not faced with their ninth graders in prior years. When the teachers came together to discuss attendance, they concluded that they were collectively seeing many more students who were struggling academically. During our interviews, the teachers described the profound benefits of this half-day meeting had on their awareness of their students. They hoped they could have these meeting more often and earlier the next year, instead of later, when they were usually "on the verge of heading toward a cliff."

Because Pompano Beach High School had already demonstrated a strong culture of personalization, PASL was a natural fit for the school. The educator team engaged in much the same way that Ely High School engaged in Cross-Talks, but Pompano Beach met much more informally. Specifically, the team members would gather the range of student information (goals, grades, etc.) from the school's database. PASL teachers also used this gift of time to identify students who needed to be referred to intervention. Interesting things would come up when a student's PASL teachers met with other teachers the student had but who were not part of

PASL. The PASL teachers would see how a student was doing in the other classes as well. This meeting time enabled both PASL and non-PASL teachers to see that some students might be shutting down in one class but might be very animated in another. This interaction provided a space for the teachers to discuss ideas and brainstorm what they could do to help that student become more engaged and motivated. As implementation progressed, the PASL teachers had data to support PASL efforts. They came together to share implementation and outcome data with the school's improvement team and the faculty.

The PASL coordinator emphasized that it took time to get all the teachers on board with PASL—with only about half the staff on board at first. Teachers who were making the reform work tried to steer the others on the right course simply by showing them their best practices and what else was working for them so far. The coordinator also noted that she worked strategically with the master scheduler to make sure the teachers with a first-period class of ninth graders would be the people most likely to agree to PASL. Some teachers were unwilling to add anything to their plates, and no teacher was contractually required to do so. Over time, however, more teachers began to see the value in PASL, and once the school established more of a structure for implementing it, by the third year, more teachers were on board and willing to participate.

Conclusion

PASL did not happen overnight. In some cases, schools took several years to develop the most effective educator-team structure and routine that made the most sense for themselves. The measured pace and the district's willingness to let its schools adapt the reform for their own needs and situation is what sets both PASL and Broward County Public Schools apart from other districts trying reforms. The district and school leadership gave the schools the freedom to start small and customize PASL. Paired with ongoing support from school administration, the PASL reform made the schools even more successful, as we'll see in the next chapter.

Any school reform takes time. Part of what makes PASL unique is its focus on building relationships not only between teachers and students but also among teachers. Collaborating as teams of educators with a student-centered perspective can improve not only the learning experience for students but also the teaching experience for adults. Once teachers are supported with the time and resources to engage in these key activities collectively, then and only then can they begin the critical work of personalizing the education of their students in meaningful and collaborative ways with their colleagues.

Educator teams can take various forms, but they must have specific features to provide the time for teachers and other staff to come together to talk about students and PASL practices. By having a space where they can meet, teachers build connections with each other and receive support from peers around similar concerns and questions. Although the intent for the educator collaboration around PASL was to provide a time devoted to discussions about students, we found that along the way, the collaboration also strengthened the relationships between teachers and led to a stronger adult school community built on conversations and trust.

CHAPTER 7

Component 5: CULTURES OF PERSONALIZATION

Environments Where Students Feel Seen and Heard

Charles W. Flanagan High School is an example of a school whose commitment to a high-quality student experience runs high among the adults. Located in the southeastern section of Broward County, not far from the Everglades and the Miami-Dade County border, Flanagan High School has an enrollment of approximately three thousand students, with 48 percent of students identifying as Latinx, 33 percent as Black, 13 percent as White, and 6 percent as other. Slightly over half of the students qualify for free and reduced-price lunch. Administrators, counselors, and teachers seek to create a warm and embracing culture at the school. The school itself is welcoming, with a large courtyard in front of the cafeteria and media center displaying student art and with college banners lining the ceiling. Students travel between classrooms outside in the warm Florida temperatures. They eat lunch in the school's courtyard, where it is common to hear bands play or music blasting for a dance troupe. Students are friendly, saying hello to adults in the hallways. With its broad mission of "A Quality School Providing More than an Education," Flanagan High School provides a friendly and academic environment for students.

In conducting our research with Broward County Public Schools, we visited Flanagan High School four times during our visits to the district, with the visits ranging from one to five days. In our interviews and other interactions over the years, the educators at Flanagan consistently described the students at their school as young people who were there to make friends, develop their interests and skills, and figure out what they wanted to do after graduation. Academics were important—the school was highly attuned to its Florida accountability grade and student performance—but so were the social aspects of students' lives. One school administrator explained that the school made a concerted effort to focus on "the child as a whole." Administrators and teachers at Flanagan decided to implement PASL with all ninth graders. Rapid check-ins would occur in second period, and students would do the goal-achievement lessons with their physical education teachers. The configuration changed over the years, with teachers conducting the rapid check-ins and goal-achievement lessons in different periods, but the school never wavered in its clear identity as a welcoming place for growing adolescents. While students in other grades were not the main focus of PASL, there was the expectation that the culture of personalization would permeate the entire school.

CHARLES W. FLANAGAN HIGH SCHOOL: BUILDING ON
THE FUNDAMENTALS

Many fundamentals of a culture of personalization were already in place when Flanagan started implementing PASL in 2014, the first year of the implementation in the district. As described by a teacher leader, "The principal's vision is built around relationships, and so when she comes in and says this is what I believe in, there's a lot of techniques that she's instilled in the school to build and foster relationships among the teachers, the students, the parents, the community." When we spoke with adults at the end of the first year of implementation, they described PASL as consistent with what they had already been doing in terms of general approach and activities. They said that PASL helped nudge the school's culture to one of personalization, strengthening the quality of support for students at the school. The principal, Michelle Kefford, had started a mentoring program called Kefford's Kids the year before. As part of the mentoring program, administrators, guidance counselors, and teachers identified incoming ninth-grade students who the adults believed would benefit from the one-on-one mentoring activities. The administrators then asked highly involved eleventh- and twelfth-grade students to serve as peer mentors to these ninth graders. The mentors were expected to check in on students regularly, and once a semester, the school sponsored a social event for Kefford's Kids.

One such event occurred when we were visiting. It had a Hawaiian theme, and the adults dressed in colorful shirts and presented funny skits for the students. As part of the fun, the teens were treated to snow cones. One teacher explained that the logic of Kefford's Kids included goals embodied in PASL: "So rather than just helping the kids academically, we realized that the personalization—that mentoring piece between the kids—also had a big effect [on the ninth graders] and then with the mentors as well."

The administrators and teachers expressed belief in PASL as an approach to help improve student outcomes and increase their sense of belonging at the school. These beliefs served as the foundation for the school's culture of personalization, which teacher described in different ways. One teacher explained that PASL "has a tremendous impact because when [students] know that you care about them, not just academically as desks, but when they really know that you're engaged and you know them and want to know them even at a personal level, they want to give to you." Another said that her belief in PASL came from seeing improvements in students' grades and test scores: "People believe in it . . . Like for us alone, our data speaks for itself." For some adults, PASL resonated as a concept, but others were convinced when they saw its impact on students and their performance.

The teachers also communicated the importance of PASL in multiple ways, putting the students' well-being at the center of the reform. One way teachers demonstrated the importance of PASL was through the regularly scheduled professional-development meetings. The assistant principal, Brad Fatout, saw the first meeting of the year, before school began, as a way to set the tone for the rest of the year. He explained that he had introduced PASL "to the whole faculty during pre-planning so they're all aware of PASL. I share the information on how we motivate the students, what the PASL students are doing in their second period, what the team is doing with the whole faculty. So I try to keep that communication ongoing so it's live. So if a teacher who is teaching tenth, eleventh, and twelfth graders is intrigued about something that we're doing, they might use similar strategies." Administrators and teacher leaders explained that by emphasizing PASL as they began the school year, the other teachers became aware of how much these school leaders valued it.

The school leadership also took the same introductory approach with students through a motivational assembly at the beginning of the school year. During this assembly of ninth-grade students, Kefford and Fatout shared their vision for the year and talked about the need for students to do the right thing and make good choices. Another way that adults built connections with students was through athletics, clubs, and other programs. Over 70 percent of the students already participated in extracurricular activities at the school.

Over the years of implementation, the administrators and teachers made some changes to how they implemented PASL. For example, in the second year, the adults thought that teachers new to the reform needed more support. Five teachers with a strong knowledge of PASL became "PASL Pals" to the newly implementing teachers. Administrators and PASL teachers saw the use of peer experts as a professional learning strategy for teachers of ninth-grade students. Here, a select group of high-adopting teachers served as mentors for the other ninth-grade teachers to "parlay information" from the administrators and teacher leaders to teachers in the classroom. One teacher leader explained: "We'll reach out to them so that we make sure that we're reaching out to every PASL teacher. Now again with schedules and everything else, the conversations have to be short, condensed . . . It's usually about rapid check-in, but at least they know, if I just want to say something to somebody about this or there's another person I can talk to."

We spoke to several students at Flanagan during our visits. In these discussions, each student described an adult at the school who the teen felt comfortable talking to every day if the student needed to do so. The teachers communicated a general culture of personalization and caring in many ways. For some students, there were indications of general caring when teachers "were friendly." There were also gestures of academic support such as providing extra-credit opportunities, "helping bring up my grade," and directing students to peer tutoring. One student said that one teacher had "always been there for me, personally." Another explained that a coach "empowers me to play football." A girl said that her math teacher was "like a mother." Another student appreciated when a teacher held high expectations for him. While students said that not all teachers showed this level of caring, at least one or two teachers for each of them did.

The students also talked about being involved in the school and in extracurricular activities. In one focus group, a student said, "Everybody I know does something." Students described having many options. One student said, "They have, like, everything for everybody." They described being in different programs, such as color guard, a program for high school students interested in becoming teachers, wrestling, football, the Hispanic Student Association, and the Humane Society's Pets Are Worth Saving.

To summarize, administrators and teachers at Flanagan High School sought to create a personalizing culture at the school. Led by the school administration and teacher leaders, the school set an overall tone of caring for students while encouraging extracurricular activities and athletics. Through the principal's sponsored peer mentoring program that infused fun into an effort to build relationships between students, PASL students could feel engaged and appreciated at the school.

Features of a Culture of Personalization

A culture of personalization is the fifth component of PASL. It strives to make school personal for students. When schools have such a culture, educators engage in norms, activities, and behaviors that signal to students that the school is a place where each of them matters. Cultures of personalization are built on small gestures and conversations that individuals engage in throughout the school day and communicate that people at the school matter. Teachers build cultures of personalization when they greet students at the door and acknowledge students in the hallway through a smile and a nod. Administrators invest in a culture of personalization when they joke and chat with students in the cafeteria during lunch, showing that they are not disciplinarians, but rather role models. When adults engage in these types of daily interactions, they create an environment where students feel seen and heard.

Cultures of personalization are associated not only with norms of behavior and daily interactions, but also with specific practices and programs that cultivate positive and constructive adult-student relationships, such as mentoring program and extracurricular activities. For example, teachers can tailor a lesson or unit around student interests to relate a concept or an event to students' lives and experiences. In this way, the teachers make the subject matter culturally relevant to students. Rapid check-ins and goal-achievement lessons are another part of the culture. Adults create cultures of personalization, therefore, by modeling behavior, "effortful engagement," and programs and practices that provide a structure for students to grow.[1] They are built through the system of personalization of PASL. Put differently, the other components contribute to a culture of personalization, but a culture of personalization must also be attended to.

Norms are also built through the visual landscape of the school. Does the school look welcoming? Is it painted and clean? Is it an attractive place that clearly reflects the students' interests and activities? Are all areas safe? Communicating a sense of welcome to students can include colorful, attractive posters about clubs and activities and trophy cases where past students are acknowledged for their athletic and scholastic successes. The presence of adults in hallways and other school areas also conveys to students that adults are taking care of the students.

Schools also engage in practices that build interpersonal connections and directly signal to students that they matter. Among the thirty-one schools that participated in the PASL reform, we

have seen schools do various activities that foster a culture of personalization. Some schools have structured their communication
with students in a way that makes adults more accessible and
worth listening to. For example, announcements over the public
address system and on the school website have presented adults
in a friendlier, open way than is typical at schools. We have seen
schools use surveys with students to gather their input on different
topics. Some schools we observed used assemblies to communicate
PASL concepts and values to students. These assemblies have included sessions to help ninth graders understand how to calculate
their GPA, sessions on the impact of their grades on college acceptance, and talks by a motivational speaker. The schools have sought
to make extracurricular activities easily available to students. The
schools we studied have organized pizza parties, ice cream socials,
celebratory luncheons, and other celebrations where students feel
appreciated and valued.

These are all different ways in which adults and students communicate with each other and ways for adults in schools to show
students that they care about them. What matters is the underlying understanding between the adults and the students that they
treat each other well. In these kinds of environments, students feel
acknowledged.

Research on Cultures of Personalization

School cultures are important. As education researchers Kent Peterson and Terrence Deal describe them, cultures are "the under-
ground stream of norms, values, beliefs, traditions, and rituals that
has built up over time as people work together, solve problems,
and confront challenges. This set of informal expectations and
values shapes how people think, feel, and act in schools."[2] Abun-
dant research supports the importance of positive school cultures.

Studies have found that they shape students' sense of connection to their school and teachers' longevity at a school. School cultures shape students' behavior and school safety. They can set clear expectations regarding bullying and the well-being of lesbian, gay, bisexual, transgender, and queer students. They also improve students' developmental outcomes.[3]

At their core, cultures of personalization are about building relationships between people in schools. With PASL, adults at a school make an additional effort to provide an environment in which relationships thrive for both adults and students. They seek to implement norms, values, and rituals that reinforce the importance of communication, mutual respect, and shared interests. Through the ways that they interact with students, adults communicate that they want to help them succeed and achieve their goals. They convey that they care about students. Adolescents are seen not just as students, but also as whole people. Strong relationships build trust between adults and students, adults and adults, and students and students and constitute an essential component of effective schools.[4]

As discussed, the importance of personalization in schools is not a new idea. In the 1990s, personalization in schools gained traction as way to improve schools.[5] One reformer, Timothy Dyer, argued, "If schools don't implement this one, there will be no reform."[6] For those advocating for personalization in the 1990s, it was almost exclusively about creating a school culture that promoted students' sense of belonging and connections between adults and students. They argued that personalized school environments led to stronger schools: "For students of all degrees of academic involvement," Milbrey W. McLaughlin and coauthors wrote, "personal bonds with adults in the school have a greater capacity to motivate and engage than do traditional forms of social control that emphasize obedience to authority and conformity to rules."[7] They said that not only do personalized environments benefit students, but this personalization also benefits the adults, who feel at a disadvantage when they do not know their students. For these researchers, studies of schools and classrooms depicted schools "as impersonal, harsh and competitive [with] little attachment between teachers and students." They underscored that schools benefit when they cultivate a personalized environment through deliberate choices about how to organize their routines and activities and emphasize the importance of communication and collegial support. Through these decisions, schools structure the very nature of the relationships between and among adults and students.

We now turn briefly to our original research on the four case study high schools, exploring what made some high schools in Broward County more effective than others. As discussed earlier, we found that personalization made the difference.[8] It permeated the higher performing schools through organizational design and routines and through the ways that adults communicated to students that they, the students, were important. In these schools, administrators, teachers, guidance counselors, and other staff promoted a culture of personalization in the ways that they actively shared norms about how to engage both formally and informally with students. Students knew that there were at least two adults in the school —their class administrator and counselor—who were there throughout their time at the school. Students felt welcome and heard by various adults in the school, such as the teachers who tailored the content of their daily lessons to students' interests and the principal at weekly student lunches.

We also discovered the importance of being intentional and consistent about a culture of personalization. Such a culture requires effort. At the lower performing schools, there were, of course, adults who cared about their students and sought to have constructive interactions. However, we found that their efforts to interact with students were less purposeful. Compared with the adults in higher performing schools, these adults were less likely to identify personal connections as a priority and instead focused on the barriers to positive relationships. Several adults were frustrated at the school, perceived a lack of follow-through by administrators, complained about inconsistent disciplinary procedures, and spoke of favoritism. Adults often identified the students and their parents as the root cause for the dysfunction they the teachers were feeling, complaining about poor attitudes and behavior and a failure of the parents to hold their children to high standards. Our study underscored the importance of personalization as an effective strategy.

Other educators' research also supports the importance of a culture of personalization. Peterson and Deal found that schools that do not attend to a culture of personalization risk becoming toxic, "where staffs are extremely fragmented, where the purpose of serving students has been lost to the goal of serving the adults, where negative values and hopelessness reign."[9] To be sure, work in schools can be discouraging and dispiriting when students come unprepared for class, are unfocused, and disrupt instruction. However, adults experiencing these feelings must ask themselves if they are willing to change their dynamics with students. Students, for their part, are clear about what constitutes a "good" and "bad" teacher. "Good" teachers are fair, treat them like adults, explain things clearly, spend time helping, and are considerate of student feelings. In contrast, "bad" teachers are "dull, boring, don't explain things clearly, show favoritism toward students and have a poor attitude."[10] With these basic attitudes of fairness and trust, administrators, teachers, and other adults communicate that students are important.

Additional studies point to the importance of different elements of school culture. Studies have long found that schools with strong visions, missions, and culture around shared values and beliefs have a strong positive impact on student learning.[11] In these environments, explain Douglas Breunlin and his colleagues, schools have "structures, policies, and practices that promote relationships based on mutual respect, trust, collaboration, and support."[12] School leaders have a role to play in setting the overall tone and making sure that the entire school staff and students feel supported. They set a supportive tone when they attend to their interactions with school stakeholders, including students, parents, community members, and the other adults who work in the building. If relationships are at the center of personalization, school leaders must support and encourage numerous types of relationships: teacher-student, student-student, teacher-teacher, community-school, parent-teacher, faculty-administration, and so forth. With these relationships, school leaders set to model the kind of interactions that they feel best reflect the values and culture of their school.

If relationships are at the core of a culture of personalization, research has also found that leaders need to pay attention to the nature of these relationships. While students are required to go to school until age sixteen, we can hope that people who work in schools are motivated by an interest and desire to interact with adolescents at an important time in their lives. Schools have long been understood as systems of interpersonal relationships, with the goal of educational attainment.[13] Adults show caring when they express interest in students' lives, both academically and socially. A personalized school environment promotes "an ethic of caring" and "a relational ethic" in which students not only feel cared for, but also develop critical interpersonal social skills with peers, teachers, and the school community at large.[14] When adults are engaged with their students and show this caring, students' sense of belonging and engagement in their own learning is improved. Furthermore, cultures of personalization also attend to the student-student relationship; healthy socialization occurs in environments where students feel comfortable.[15]

For all students, quality relationships are important. Each student comes to school with different needs. The relationships formed in high school are as central to adolescent development as is academic learning, particularly in light of studies that show that social-emotional competencies are critical to college and career success.[16] Adults in schools tend to be more comfortable in their instructional role, particularly in this era of assessment and accountability, and less clear on their role of providing social and emotional support to students.[17] Schools that foster a culture of personalization actively help adults cultivate their relationships with students, whether it is through routines such as rapid check-ins, reminding teachers about modeling different kinds of social interactions, or other more direct strategies. In turn, these relationships help build the students' knowledge, skills, and social competencies that are critical for college and the workforce.

All schools provide support either informally through these relationships or formally through different services, such as guidance and college and career planning. Some students will actively take advantage of these services, while others will rely on them to a lesser degree. Some students, however, will require additional support to get through high school. For these students, one-on-one interactions with adults at school are particularly important. While many students have strong, functional adults at home encouraging them, others do not. Adults play a particularly important role for vulnerable students who are at higher risk of dropping out, such as low-income students, students of color, and English language learners. Adults can model these interpersonal skills, but they can also actively promote them as they make sure that these students get the help they need.

In addition to the norms of practice and language, there are also well-documented activities that schools can use to intentionally promote a culture of personalization. Students who participate in extracurricular activities, such as sports and school clubs, experience numerous benefits, including higher academic achievement and greater engagement at their school, although the advantages may differ by school.[18] These students are also more likely to go to college.[19] Through extracurricular activities, students are exposed to ambitious peers and a work ethic applied to something besides academics. Athletic coaches, band directors, ROTC sergeants, advisers of the student government association are all examples of structured role models outside the classroom. Besides enjoying academic rewards, students who participate in extracurricular activities also exhibit greater persistence, grit, and social skills.[20]

Another activity that promotes cultures of personalization is mentoring. Mentoring programs signal to students that there is another adult or an older student at the school who is there to give them one-on-one attention and guidance.[21] Much like the adults conducting the rapid check-ins, mentors are, at their best, another source of social-emotional support for the student. Studies on adult mentoring programs show that they are effective ways to improve students' GPAs, promote high school completion, and decrease dropout rates.[22] Peer mentoring programs benefit both the mentee and the mentor, increasing both participants' self-esteem and connection to the school. Studies also emphasize that these programs must provide training to mentors and work best if they are included as part of an overall community effort.[23]

Tailoring Systems of Personalization

Effective schools work as coherent systems with visions, missions, organizational routines, and cultures that bridge the academic, social-emotional, and behavioral elements of schooling.[24] But how do schools build linkages between these elements? Throughout this book, we have described how we identified and developed PASL. We explained our process of improvement and each component of the reform. In our discussions, we have shown how each component interacts with different components, but we have not yet emphasized how PASL works as a system of components. We now turn to two schools what do just this. That is, we explain how each school built its culture of personalization both as a stand-alone component and through the system of PASL.

POMPANO BEACH HIGH SCHOOL: BALANCING RIGOR AND STRESS

At Pompano Beach High School, located thirty miles from Flanagan High School, we observed a different approach to a culture of personalization, one built on a different school mission and vision. As we described in earlier chapters, Pompano Beach is a school for students who have shown a certain level of grade and test score performance. Students describe pressure to perform well. The year the school signed on to implement PASL, the administration and students had identified the problem of inordinate amounts of academic stress on students. The prior year, too many students had failed to meet the school's academic requirements. A counselor said that the academic focus created a challenge; teachers were "so focused on their curriculum, they fail to see the emotional needs of the child." Both the adults and the students reported a strong culture of high expectations, but for some students, the expectations were too high. The people we interviewed generally agreed that the school had lost sight of its purpose. Not only should the school prepare high performing students for college, but it should also make sure that students felt a connection to the school and were engaged in other activities that boosted their self-esteem and sense of belonging. Administrators, guidance counselors, and teachers turned to PASL in an effort to balance the school's strong focus on academics.

At the same time, as a second-year adopter, Pompano Beach administrators decided to implement a version of Kefford's Kids from Flanagan High School at the school after learning about it at a PASL network meeting. Consequently, the school's approach represented both its own organic representation of a culture of personalization and one with features adopted from other schools.

With the school's strong focus on academic success, PASL at Pompano Beach needed to be consistent with the school's academic mission. During the first year of implementing PASL, the school chose the head counselor and a ninth-grade counselor on the implementation team. Because of their input, the school's approach to PASL generally—and the culture of personalization specifically—centered on the support students needed to be successful both in and out of the classroom. As Lori Carlson, the ninth-grade guidance counselor, explained, "PASL is a program designed for teachers to make a conscious effort to connect on a personal level with their students. I feel the goal should be that teachers are making that effort every day, but understand that curriculum and requirements may get in the way where you really just have to focus on what you need to do. But making that connection with students gets them involved in the school, increases productivity, and provides a better learning environment for the students in your class."

As one of the first scale-out schools, Pompano Beach was able to learn from the experiences of the first three schools when it implemented PASL. It gravitated toward Flanagan's peer mentoring model as a structure to foster a culture of personalization. However, whereas Flanagan focused on building relationships between student leaders and identified ninth graders, the leadership team at Pompano Beach decided to build on its mentoring program in which each ninth-grade student was paired with a junior or senior. Students met with their peer mentors once a month on a Wednesday. Over the school year, the school organized different peer mentoring events and organized sessions where the older students taught specific lessons that they thought ninth graders needed to know. In one of these sessions that we observed, ninth-grade students and their mentors traveled in small groups to different stations presenting different scenarios, including plagiarism and drugs on campus. At each station, the teens stopped to discuss the central issue in the scenario.

The students at Pompano Beach were a loud and vocal group who did not hold back when we interviewed them. The ninth graders all agreed that there were teachers at the school they could talk to. Among the comments were "I like her personality; she's cool," "they'll give you advice," and "she just wants what's best for you and is really kind." All the students could describe the types of support they were receiving at the school. For example, they got help with calculating their GPA, choosing the best classes according to their grades, and setting and achieving goals. These students distinguished between the "genuine" teachers and the "rude and condescending" ones who didn't learn their names, showed favoritism, and called them out in front of the whole class. Many of the students' criticisms focused on impeding students from academic success. Students complained that two teachers were late in posting grades until the end of the quarter, "so you don't know what you have to make up." A student described a teacher as holding students to "a really unrealistic standard, because she's like, 'You wouldn't be here if you couldn't handle it. If you can't handle it, you don't deserve to be here.'" For these students, the school's academic focus only put more pressure on them. They could easily identify the teachers who they felt supported them and those who had more of a "gotcha" approach.

Pompano Beach's aim with PASL, therefore, has been to provide support for students in an academically rigorous environment. Through the school's rapid check-ins and goal-achievement lessons, administrators, teachers, and counselors have been implementing PASL since 2015. Over the years, the school has continued to build on the mentor program, providing students with monthly informational sessions around topics such as goal setting, stress management, and the college entrance process. The school conducts social-emotional check-in surveys with students twice a year, taking the temperature of students' attitudes and concerns. It has also experimented with the frequency that peer mentors meet with students. In the first year of implementation, the peer mentors met with the students at least twice a month. The following year, the school decided to arrange weekly check-ins but, by 2018, had decided on once a month. In addition to the mentoring, Pompano Beach discusses PASL during a presentation to both incoming students and their parents.

In 2017, one of the school leaders explained that the peer mentoring program had helped students have greater ownership over their learning and had encouraged schoolwide PASL, as students moved up from ninth grade and became mentors themselves. This leader believed that when teachers observed the students' positive responses to PASL, the adults were convinced of its value as well.

Both Pompano Beach and Flanagan built strong cultures of personalization, even though the schools responded differently to the needs of their particular population of students. Both presented a warm, welcoming environment, however. Flanagan honored the broad interests of the student body, whereas Pompano Beach focused on its mission as an academic community. At Flanagan, the adults believed that it was important to support identified students, providing them with strong mentorship with high performing juniors and seniors. Pompano Beach implemented the mentorship program for all ninth graders to help them feel a sense of belonging and a connection with an older student, and in so doing, the school included more of the juniors and seniors. Both schools developed approaches that met the needs of their school community.

CORAL SPRINGS HIGH SCHOOL: AN INTEGRATED SYSTEM OF SUPPORTS

Coral Springs High School, which was in the fourth cohort of Broward County high schools to begin implementing PASL, also demonstrates how this reform works as a system. The school's PASL team, spearheaded by its assistant principal, Tameka King, decided to have three personalization periods in which teachers would participate in PASL (the number has since been expanded to twenty-two). Unlike some schools that targeted low performing students, the team at Coral Springs decided that each personalization period would include students across academic achievement levels, recognizing that all students could benefit from PASL. During the personalization periods, the PASL teachers conducted informal rapid check-ins with students but, every two or three weeks, aimed to have a lengthier discussion with the students. The assistant principal provided the teachers with an optional FileMaker Pro link to document the rapid check-ins.

The PASL teachers also worked with students on their goal-achievement activities. The students identified both short-term goals, such as improving their grades or joining a club, and long-term goals, such as identifying a college to attend. During their formal check-ins with the students, the teachers would, if appropriate, return to these goals. The guidance counselor used Naviance to help students identify goals and shared them with the teachers. Through the routine check-ins and the goal-setting activities, the teachers gained a greater depth of knowledge about the students, including their successes and challenges. By knowing the students' goals, the adults could make sure their interactions with the students always related to these goals.

While the teachers were generating data through their rapid check-ins and the goal-achievement activities, the assistant principal made monthly reports of the students' data for each personalization teacher. The teachers used these reports to follow up, through a rapid check-in, with struggling students who needed additional resources. They also used the data to recognize students for positive outcomes such as improvements in their grades or behavior and to provide recognition and support. In this way, teachers, guidance counselors, and administrators used multiple sources of data, some generated through their own interactions, some obtained through the school's online data system or Naviance, and some provided by the assistant principal.

Two or three times per quarter, the teachers met in educator teams before the school day to discuss PASL activities and the students. At the beginning of the year, they discussed PASL strategies and their implementation. Members of this team also rotated attendance at the district network meetings, so that each teacher could participate at some point in the year as part of the school's PASL team. The teachers' participation in these district meetings helped instill their identities as PASL teachers and empowered them to be part of designing the reform at Coral Springs.

Many people spoke of how the assistant principal walked through the hallways asking students how they were doing in an effort to build a culture of personalization. Adults and students alike discussed a culture of "doing their best" and efforts to recognize students through events and awards. Students also said that after-school tutoring was another way that the adults provided support to students. A self-professed student-centered leader, the principal also described efforts to respect teachers' professional judgement both in and out of the classroom, believing that this would help teachers make stronger connections.

Individually, each activity and routine at Coral Springs High School either builds a connection with another person (e.g., rapid check-ins and educator teams) or provides information to further relationships in the school (e.g., goal-achievement activities and the use of data). All of this is conducted within a culture of personalization that supports and reinforces these practices. While these systems do not necessarily work flawlessly, and although the school started small with highly engaged teachers, Coral Springs has successfully built a system in which adults and students feel that others in the school are listening to them.

Conclusion

Practitioners, reformers, and researchers have known for several decades that cultures of personalization make a difference in schools. These cultures emerge from systems of routines and practices that, when done well, build trust between educators, students, and the entire school community. The cultures are deliberately built through greetings in the hallway, jokes in the cafeteria, welcoming spaces, mentoring programs, tutoring, speakers, and extracurricular activities. A personalization culture requires effortful engagement across all stakeholders. The PASL reform offers a model for personalization—a model that bridges the classroom and the school. The reform provides a structure for schools to adapt to their own circumstances. Ultimately, it is up to administrators, teachers, guidance counselors, and other educators to work with students to build their own unique culture.

CHAPTER 8

WHY PASL WORKS

Building on What High Schools Are Already Doing

Serving students with a wide variety of interests and academic levels, American high schools have had mixed results meeting the needs of all students. They still retain elements from their development in the early twentieth century, when having students attend multiple courses across a school day was seen as a way to efficiently educate a large and diverse population. Reformers have argued that it is difficult to meet the needs of all adolescents with the traditional model, yet high schools have remained committed to it. The schools are often compared to factories, with the implication that students and adults move through respective roles, producing their outputs.[1] In this depiction, high schools are cast as harsh places where students come to study and graduate, with their social and emotional elements secondary to academics. Efforts to restructure high schools away from this traditional model toward one more sensitive to the needs of different students, such as interdisciplinary teaching or removing tracks, have been met with skepticism and pushback from multiple stakeholders, including administrators, teachers, and parents.

In this book, we have described an approach to high school reform whose fundamental purpose is to bridge schools' academic and social-emotional components by harnessing the practices and systems already present in the traditional high school model. At its core, Personalization for Academic and Social-Emotional Learning (PASL) improves the quality of the relationships between students and adults. It aims to move schools to places where students and adults feel listened to and valued. Through five components, schools strengthen the routines and practices that are already in place. Students and adults may enter high schools as individuals, each with his or her own interests, personalities, and skills, but they must come together to come together to create a culture. High schools must be understood as vibrant social environments where adults and students come not only to participate in academic learning but also to interact with, and relate to, each other. When understood in this way, both the academic and the social purposes of school are acknowledged and the important role that relationships play in supporting the fundamental work of schools is emphasized. This perspective not only casts schools as joyful places but also recognizes a central reality of adolescents and adults, namely, that they are interdependent and thrive from strong personal connections.

In this final chapter, we discuss the importance of PASL as a system of practices working to improve routines and relationships in schools. PASL will be examined within the history of high school reforms, where it can be understood in the context of long-standing debates about the purposes of American high schools. We also reflect on the reform approach of continuous improvement as a mechanism for change, particularly on why PASL has been successful in Broward County Public Schools. There are, of course, challenges to the model, some that we have addressed and others that remain. This chapter will look at important lessons that we hope will help others interested in adapting PASL to other schools and districts.

PASL in the Landscape of High School Reform

Reforming high schools is not a new idea in the United States. High schools have retained a form and structure for over a hundred years, and although there have been efforts to transform high schools, they have remained largely resistant to significant structural changes. Yet while their organization has remained remarkably consistent, there have been ongoing debates for over a century about their goals and purpose for adolescents. Historians of education have documented eras where reformers call for high academic expectations and rigor for students. They also identified times that called for high schools to be more attentive to the needs of different students across ability levels to help them develop attitudes and skills as they make the transition into adulthood, postsecondary opportunities, and the workforce.[2] To understand how PASL works, we need to understand it in the larger context of high schools and the debates about their purpose.

Origins of the Modern High School: Conflicting Aims

The modern American high school—with its curricular differentiation and with its students organized by age, traveling from class to class every hour, and enrolled in five to seven courses led by subject-matter experts—became commonplace in the early twentieth century. One hundred years later, students still receive Carnegie units, which denote the completion of 120 contact hours in a course. Through Carnegie units, high schools provide students with a validated curricular experience and signal to postsecondary institutions that the students have met the stated requirements.[3] With the highest rate of high school graduation ever at 85 percent in 2017, completion has become a rite of passage for most students, one that promises financial and social rewards for those receiving a diploma.[4] Yet many students express feelings of alienation from high school, and only a minority are graduating with the academic skills needed for college.[5] High schools still have room for improvement to address the needs of today's adolescents.

Throughout the twentieth century, high school enrollment and graduation grew. As more adolescents attended high school, reformers debated if high school should retain its original academic focus or if its purpose should extend beyond the conferral of academic credentials. During the Progressive Era, the National Education Association's Commission on the Reorganization of Secondary Education called for high schools to serve the broader goals of socialization, preparing students for "work, family life, good health, citizenship, ethical character, and worthy use of leisure."[6] These reformers called for greater differentiation between students according to their aptitude and interests; institutionalizing tracking as a feature of high schools; and a diversity of course content, ranging from home economics to physical education to calculus, to acknowledge students' different interests and career goals. Multiple tracks emerged: academic, commercial, general, and vocational.[7]

As the United States emerged from World War II, a new generation of reformers, fueled by Cold War anxieties, began a renewed interest in academic rigor. Concerned with remaining internationally competitive, particularly in the sciences, these reformers called for a "revamping of the curricula, tougher selection and training of teachers, greater regimentation in the classroom, attention to patriotism and fewer 'frills.'"[8] With the Russian launch of *Sputnik* in 1957, reformers only intensified the focus on academic rigor, deriding high school education as having a weak curriculum and being in decline. The reformers particularly focused on high performing students in mathematics, science, and languages.[9]

Over the last sixty years, debates about high schools have reflected these familiar arguments. In the 1960s and 1970s, with the focus on universal access and addressing racial, gender, and socioeconomic inequalities, reformers called for high schools to meet the needs of all students, adding remedial courses to the curriculum and more progressive pedagogy.[10] Schools hired guidance counselors to help students navigate through their courses and to make available an adult at the school to talk about the students' social and emotional concerns.[11] During the early 1980s, however, two commissions set their gaze on American high schools, with ramifications that continue to this day. Motivated by similar concerns about their nature, effectiveness, and broad mission, both commissions raised anxieties about the failure of high schools to meet students' academic needs. Despite this similar focus, they came to different conclusions on how to remedy the problems.

Two Approaches to Reform

In 1983, President Ronald Reagan's National Commission on Excellence in Education published a report on the status of US education. Titled "A Nation at Risk," the report called for clearer academic guidelines, higher curricular standards, more time in school, and higher standards for teachers. It also recommended a rigorous curriculum for all students, even those "who do not plan to go to college," in addition to greater accountability and improved professionalization of teaching.[12] Educational researchers point to "A Nation at Risk" as the rallying cry for the standards and assessment movement that has driven federal and state policy for the last thirty-five years. Through the 1990s and the 2000s, the federal policies of Goals 2000, No Child Left Behind, and

Race to the Top—fueled by anxieties about keeping up internationally—slowly institutionalized standards, assessments, and data systems to track students. State-level policies such as minimum-competency exams, the grading of high schools according to student graduation rates, the Common Core State Standards, and participation in AP courses and International Baccalaureate have further solidified an academic push. These policies have reinforced the academic focus in high schools, with teachers incentivized to increase academic rigor.[13]

A joint study by the National Association of Secondary School Principals and the Commission on Educational Issues of the National Association of Independent Schools, in contrast, called for a broad reimagining of the American high school. Led by Theodore Sizer, a well-respected secondary school principal and former dean of the Harvard Graduate School of Education, the joint team conducted five years of observational and historical inquiries into the state of the American high school. In three volumes, Sizer summarized the group's findings: that high schools across the country were similar in their form, structure, rituals, and tensions. In the first volume in the series, *Horace's Compromise*, Sizer summarized these commonalities: "High school is a kind of secular church, a place of national rituals that mark stages of a young citizen's life . . . Tacit agreement exists as to the purpose of high school and how it is to be accomplished."[14]

Across the three volumes, the authors called for a reenvisioning of high schools as places that addressed increased rigor but that also sought to engage adults and students more meaningfully through approaches such as mastery learning, greater adult-student interaction, and faculty governance. The educators argued that although high schools had the potential to be engaging and meaningful places, most were in fact the opposite, overly reliant on bureaucracy and staffed by stressed and demoralized teachers without the time or energy to truly engage students. Sizer would go on to start a national reform movement called the Coalition of Essential Schools (CES), which called on participating schools to restructure by embracing nine common principles and adapting them to their local context.[15] The CES operated from 1984 to 2016.

The implementation of PASL accepts the fundamental and enduring conventional organization of high schools underscored in "A Nation at Risk." It further recognizes that schools are nested in a federal, state, and district context that is attending to high academic standards and rigor. Indeed, test-based accountability, with its standardized state tests and grading of high schools in Florida, is taken for granted in the school landscape and something that all the schools in the Broward County Public Schools must address. At the same time, as articulated by Sizer and his colleagues, PASL seeks to enhance the curricular and instructional experience of teachers by acknowledging that learning occurs in a social context. Put simply, those implementing PASL do so within the dominant organization of the American high school and, rather than try to restructure the school, work within its traditional routines, structures, and academic expectations to improve the quality of education for students.

Yet, while PASL was not developed with the CES explicitly in mind, the reform clearly shares many of the same core characteristics. One of the nine principles of the CES is personalization, which the coalition conceptualizes more as a pedagogical imperative than as building student-teacher relationships broadly. How schools adapt the common principles to their own situation is another obvious parallel. In its later years, the CES also embraced continuous school improvement as a way to structure reform.[16] A continuous-improvement model acknowledges that schools are dynamic places that are driven by the relationships guiding each interaction and that focus on the academic and social needs of children.

When viewed through this historical perspective, PASL can be understood as a reform that harnesses conventional organizational structures and routines within high schools and speaks to both their academic and their social purposes. PASL works within the existing administrative and pedagogical arrangements by focusing on the nature and quality of the relationships between individuals within schools. It employs routines that most adults in schools already use, drawing on many features that have been well established in high schools for over a century, yet seeking to strengthen and augment these features.

PASL as a System, and the Promise of Continuous Improvement

As a reform, PASL is both a set of components that schools enact as a system and an approach to school improvement. It provides a way for administrators, teachers, guidance counselors, and other school staff to work at the classrooms and school levels to strengthen organizational connections. The components of PASL help teachers make stronger connections with students in classrooms, contributing to a greater sense of belonging for students at their schools.

Adults in schools follow many of these elements of PASL already, although maybe not with the intention advocated in this book. As schools embark on their PASL journey, they need to identify and build on the programs, policies, and practices that are already in place. By building capacity in this way, schools expand on their existing strengths. Indeed, schools that build on prior capacity are much more likely to have successful reforms.[17] Not only is it easier to build on established routines and programs, but doing so also comes from an asset-based perspective rather than a deficit-based one.[18]

Though the process at Broward County Public Schools, we have also emphasized the difference between fidelity and integrity of implementation. Most school reform has been concerned with fidelity of implementation—how strictly implementers adhere to the program model and its elements such as frequency.[19] We strongly reject this vision of implementation. Through the five components of PASL, we encourage schools and their teams to think about integrity, namely, faithfulness to the components of the model, but adapting them to the local situation. With greater attention to integrity of implementation than to fidelity, schools build on their already-present strengths and routines, designing their own unique systems of personalization that meets the needs of their students and educators.

As described in chapter 2, our continuous-improvement approach to the design, implementation, and scaling of PASL reflect new ways to improve education. These approaches are proliferating because they respond to persistent challenges in school reform at scale: limited local buy-in by educators, lack of alignment with existing programs or structures in the schools, and limited time by educators to engage in the reform practices.[20] As educators know well, the traditional method of development and implementation results in a multiplicity of programs, each of which may individually be a good idea and have strong evidence behind its impact. But together, they constitute a confusing blizzard of new practices that effect little change in the core routines or relationships in schools and are not sustained as attention moves on to the next new program to be implemented.

Our continuous-improvement method was designed to overcome these challenges.[21] By building on effective practices in Broward County Public Schools and codeveloping with district educators, we hoped to build local ownership of the PASL reform and to make it adaptable to the local environment. By using the plan-do-study-act (PDSA) cycle, we learned which practices were working in which schools and how to improve those practices. And by working with a network of partners, we brought in multiple forms of expertise around a shared problem. While PASL has some differences with other emerging approaches to scale (for example, improvement science and design-based implementation research), all the methods share some common attributes.[22] First, they recognize that adaptation to context is an inevitable part of school improvement. Although we need to ensure that the changes that educators are making have good evidence behind them, we should not assume that all adaptations are bad.[23] Instead, adaptations can be tested and used to continue to improve the reform practices for the whole network. Second, all the reforms focus on the implementation itself. Decades of research on school reform indicate that implementation is not an easy process. We need to do more to support educators during the implementation of a reform, for example, giving them the time to plan, make adjustments, and keep going.

How Continuous Improvement Supports PASL at Scale

Our experience with continuous improvement suggests several underlying mechanisms that lead to success at scale. These mechanisms can support the many dimensions of scale: ownership, spread, depth, and sustainability.[24]

Ownership

Our continuous-improvement approach helped build buy-in and ownership among the educators involved in the PASL reform. By basing the design and development work on the district's needs and circumstances, and by facilitating the codevelopment of practices at the school level, we created a sense of ownership among the stakeholders. Across all phases of the work, PASL team members repeated that their direct involvement in developing the reform led to their acceptance of it. One educator summarized the collaborative nature of PASL: "This process has been, from the start, a conception of people that work in the school, that work in the district, that understand the needs and what's going on." The codevelopment approach empowered educators and fostered local leadership. This ownership is evident in how Western High School took the Cross-Talk practice from Blanche Ely High School and rebranded it in honor of Western's school mascot. The ability to adapt PASL practices to a school's own situation also fostered this sense of ownership. It allowed educators to integrate important elements of their school into their PASL practices. When Pompano Beach High School was deciding how to implement the goal-achievement lessons, for example, its peer mentoring program became something the school could plan with, rather than plan around. Blanche Ely developed the Power of Period One to enact PASL and support another school goal of improving attendance.

Spread

Another way that continuous improvement leads to success at scale comes from three ways to spread a reform: scaling in, scaling out, and scaling up. *Scaling in* focuses on deepening the implementation of a reform and maintaining its integrity to the core ideas behind the reform.[25] Implementation is the first stage of scaling in; part of achieving scale is enacting deep change in the beliefs, norms, and practices in schools.[26] Yet implementation is never really complete, and scaling in can evolve over time, perhaps deepening or establishing more sustainable infrastructure in the school. *Scaling out* is the expansion of a reform to new schools and situations. We define *scaling up* as both spreading a reform within a school and spreading it outward to new schools. By distinguishing scaling in to a school from scaling out to other schools and changing the institutional environment of the school, we emphasize that scaling up includes both horizontal and vertical aspects.[27]

Scaling out best captures the need for reforms to spread to new environments to achieve scale. Our model supported this spread through intentional formation of a network that had both school and district members. The district PASL team included members not only from the initial pilot schools, but also from the central office and other high schools in the district. These members became very important when PASL began to scale out beyond the pilot schools. Rather than having to implement PASL just as they were learning about it, three of the four first scale-out schools already had a staff member who was deeply familiar with PASL. We continued this practice as PASL continued to scale, inviting representatives from schools not expected to implement PASL until the following school year to come to network meetings. In this way, they got an early introduction to PASL and were socialized into the process of improvement. The central office members of the district PASL team were also critical. They could integrate PASL into the data warehouse through their connections with the district PASL team. The long-term involvement of the district PASL team members allowed them to be leaders in other schools and the district.

Depth

While many reforms spread to numerous schools, the changes seldom go deep. Educators may go through the motions of new practices but fail to understand the underlying ideas or logic behind them. In our model, the five PASL components and the practices within those components evolved over time. They were not formed at a single point in time and then distributed to schools as fully developed practices to implement. Each practice began as an idea based on the logic of PASL as identified in the initial research and the specific needs of a school. As school teams tried out these ideas, they gathered evidence on how the ideas were working and made adjustments to help them work better. The details of the practices shifted as school PASL teams better understood how the practices interacted with various aspects of their school. New elements were added as the teams expanded the scope of their PASL implementation, either scaling in to deepen the implementation and more fully integrate their PASL work with other elements of the school or scaling out to include more teachers and students. This type of evolution in a continuous-improvement approach builds local ownership and deepens the practitioners' understanding of the logic of PASL. Because they codeveloped PASL in their schools, the PASL team members not only knew which practices they were implementing but also understood the ideas behind them.

The evolution of data use in PASL is a good example of how practices evolved in ways that supported deeper enactment. As described in chapter 2, data use to support PASL emerged as a key theme in the original PASL strategy very early in the process. A working group was dispatched to ensure that the district's new data warehouse was responsive to PASL's data needs. Although the working group made progress in some areas, PASL's full integration with the district data system did not come until much later. At that point, Western High School was implementing PASL and realized that the school had specific data needs. Western's PASL team members could outline their data needs and prepare a mock-up for the district data system with greater specificity and usefulness than would have been possible when PASL was still in the development phase.

Sustainability

Finally, success at scale requires sustainability. Our experience shows that adaptability is inherent in continuous-improvement approaches and support sustainability. Change is a constant in public schools. For example, the community served by a school may change as the demographics shift. Or the state may pass a new education law that alters district resources or policies. Local priorities may change because of circumstances beyond the school's control. Schools are open systems that respond to their environment. In our years in working with Broward County Public Schools, we saw many changes. One reason that PASL has been sustained throughout this time is that schools could adapt to integrate the changes into the reform, rather than having to drop the reform because it no longer fit state or district policy.

Two changes were particularly important. Just as PASL was building momentum and broader support within Broward County Public Schools, the district decided to allow schools to choose whether to adopt a block schedule that includes a personalization period. The motivation for such a period was varied; PASL was one of several factors in the district's decision. After negotiations with the teacher union, it was clear that the details of the personalization period, called a study hall in some schools, did not perfectly match the needs of PASL. Some high schools chose not to adopt the personalization period. Still, this period offered many advantages for PASL, giving PASL teachers the time and space to do rapid check-ins and facilitate the goal-achievement lessons. Schools had to continue to adapt their PASL practices in the face of large changes in the structure of the school day.

Sustainability does not mean that the reform never changes. Rather, it means that commitment to, and the enactment of, the reform with integrity is maintained even as school and district priorities, resources, and other contexts shift. The adoption of the personalization period, while bringing opportunities for PASL, also represented a need to adapt the details of how PASL is implemented. The ability to continuously revise and adapt the implementation practices while maintaining integrity of the reform in the face of changing priorities and other circumstances helped to further institutionalize PASL in the schools and district.

A second threat to sustainability came through tragedy. The 2018 fatal shooting at Marjory Stoneman Douglas High School, which is part of the Broward County Public Schools, reverberated throughout the entire district. Despite its large size, Broward County is a dense network of educators. Teachers and administrators might work at one school but live in a neighboring community. Transfers between schools result in a web of personal and professional connections throughout the county. Students and staff at Stoneman Douglas experienced a very personal tragedy, but educators throughout the district also grieved for their friends, colleagues, and students. Beyond the personal ways in which the tragedy was experienced, the shooting led to changes in safety and security policies throughout the system. Broward County Public Schools educators worked long hours incorporating these new procedures. As partners with the district, we knew we had to adjust our activities in response.

Aside from mourning along with our Broward County colleagues, we adjusted to a new reality where educators had longer hours at school and increased stress as they worked to respond to each individual threat assessment. Our model empowered the schools to find ways to maintain integrity to the fundamentals of building relationships while adjusting to the new reality. Recognizing the power of student-activist voice that was raised after the shooting, one school had its PASL classes lead a series of activities to foster inclusiveness and mindfulness for their peers. Schools recognized that PASL was consistent with the needs of students and school staff, but they had to situate the reform within the heightened concern about student mental health and safety and security.

Lessons Learned

The success of our continuous-improvement approach in scaling up PASL does not mean the process was easy. We made many mistakes along the way and had to adjust elements of the model. We also had moments of serendipity, where we happened to engage with the right person at the right time. Through these mistakes and lucky breaks, we learned several lessons about how to ensure that this model would lead to improvement rather than a scattered set of practices.

Formal and Informal Leadership

Throughout the process, we learned that formal leadership matters. Successful reform comes from engaging both bureaucratic and organic forms of management. While a network-based, continuous-improvement approach does work from the bottom up, its success also stems from the structure provided from the top down. The goal is to merge bottom-up and top-down approaches to provide focus and structure while also empowering educators. Members of the district and school PASL teams liked being empowered to develop practices themselves. But they also wanted to know that what they were developing fit within the larger mission of their school and would be supported by their principal. The top-down elements of our model evolved over time. Our early efforts were hampered by a hesitancy to embrace the rational forms of management that come from the top down. Recognizing that our progress was stalling, our developer partners at the Education Development Center facilitated a "repositioning," whereby they provided more structure to the PASL teams. This structure was critical to developing PASL into a set of concrete practices that could be tested.

A second example of the need for top-down leadership was evident when two key district leaders and principal supervisors, Alan Strauss and Michael Ramirez, became committed to PASL. After seeing the results in the pilot schools, they were convinced of the power of PASL and worked to build support for it with school principals and others in the central office. They also began facilitating district PASL team meetings and framing the importance of the reform at each whole-network meeting. A principal from one of the later schools to join the network demonstrated the power of support from the leadership when he said that PASL was a "test question," meaning that when he met with his supervisor, PASL was always something he was asked about. He knew he had to be ready with a response. Merging top-down and bottom-up forms of leadership is important because we learned that ownership among levels in a district hierarchy is interrelated. While teachers and assistant principals, as individuals, may think PASL is a good idea, they were hesitant to fully commit until they saw commitment from their principal or the district. Principals, knowing how hard it would be to engage in new reforms and with many demands on their time and resources, were hesitant to fully sign on until they knew that the district central office accepted and supported the reform. And the district leaders did not want to put new mandates on schools without knowing that their principals and teachers believed in the reform. Incorporating both top-down and bottom-up approaches to leadership allowed us to build ownership across the hierarchy.

We also learned that informal leadership matters. Just as relationships between students and adults matter for student engagement and learning, relationships between educators and those who lead reform efforts matter. In most schools we worked with, the PASL coordinator was also an assistant principal. Yet a bottom-up model would seldom work if the teachers being asked to implement the practice still experienced it as another new program they were given, even if the decisions were made by an administrator at their school rather than in the central office. The most successful efforts found ways to engage teachers in leading PASL at their own schools. Another form of informal leadership is the importance of modeling the behavior you are asking others to engage in. We didn't just tell teachers to build relationships with students. Instead, we worked to build relationships and connect personally with all those who came to the network meetings. We started each meeting with music to demonstrate that serious work could also be fun, and we let people tell us what music was important to them in the process. We talked about the strengths educators bring to their work as a way to show how teachers can build on students' strengths rather than always focusing on their deficiencies. After someone wrote on a feedback form a desire for tea in addition to the morning coffee, we offered tea at the next meeting and thereafter so that the person felt heard.

Resources and Time

Like any reform effort, resources are needed to make PASL work. The most consistent theme on the feedback forms was the need for resources. The resources educators asked for came in two main varieties. One was monetary resources that they could use to support their PASL activities. For example, they suggested, funds could be used to bring in a guest speaker to motivate students. Other proposed uses for funds included a celebratory lunch or another reward for students who had achieved a goal or otherwise improved their performance and rewards for teachers who were working hard to build relationships with students. Funding was also needed to pay for professional development. During our time in Broward County, our grants provided funds for most of the professional development days, although the district covered one of the quarterly meetings. We also provided stipends for teachers to attend the annual summer institute.

A second type of resource was time. Because three of the network meetings occurred during the school day, the school had to give up teachers' time with students if the teachers were going to attend the meetings. A normal school day is packed with activity: teaching, instructional planning, grading, meeting with parents, and so forth. Teachers struggled to find time to plan for PASL and coordinate with the educator team to support students or assess PASL effectiveness. Schools used a combination of approaches, such as temporary duty assignment funds to compensate teachers for meeting after school, scheduling Cross-Talks during districtwide planning days, or carving out fifteen minutes on Academic Tuesdays.

Another element of time that we learned was important is duration. We were lucky to have partners who could see the value of PASL and the long-term benefit of our model. The story of PASL is not a one of quick wins. One of us (Dan Traeger) likes to remind us, "Be quick, but don't hurry," reflecting a belief that while we were goal-oriented, we also wanted to take the time to do things right. While the schools could point to outcomes that were improving as they engaged in PASL, it was a long road. The schools needed time to build relationships and watch those relationships lead to better results over time. Similarly, some schools occasionally lost their way in trying to remain faithful to the underlying rationale of the PASL components. Many schools embraced the idea of PASL even as they struggled to implement it in practice. Some schools made progress and then fell back. For example, despite Blanche Ely High School's successes highlighted in this book, the school experienced personnel transitions that later put PASL at risk. This type of deep change at scale takes a long time, and you need to be able to persevere through the process.

Finally, the presence of a research-practice partnership facilitated the PASL reform. We tried to honor the partnership by encouraging true synergy among all the people who helped build PASL. Partnerships come with dilemmas and challenges but also with possibilities. At various points in the reform process, we as researchers wanted to push ahead in a certain direction, but our educator partners helped us rethink the right approach. At other times, the district wanted to scale PASL more quickly than we thought was desirable. This pushing and pulling among partners happened in a system of relationships where we trusted that each party was committed to PASL and was doing the right thing for teachers and students.

Conclusion

The traditional structure of American high schools has persisted for over one hundred years, despite numerous efforts to reform it. PASL represents an approach to work within existing structures to build on what schools are doing already. This perspective is even more critical today. Students are buried behind their smartphones, anxious or dejected about their academic performance, and worried about their college and career prospects in an uncertain economy. Teachers face numerous demands and stressors, including volatile students, mountains of grading, and high-stakes testing. Administrators and guidance counselors are under pressure to meet the multiple administrative and legal demands placed on them by policy makers, parents, faculty, and students. We need to help educators become more attuned to the people in their own building and acknowledge the good work that these people are already doing. Schools are replete with such dedicated educators. By implementing and adapting PASL to the unique needs of every school, these educators can multiply their own efforts to improve the academic and social-emotional outcomes of all students.

Notes

CHAPTER 1

1. Alejandro Gaviria, and Steven Raphael. "School-Based Peer Effects and Juvenile Behavior," *Review of Economics and Statistics* 83, no. 2 (2001): 257–268.
2. David W. Johnson, "Student-Student Interaction: The Neglected Variable in Education," *Educational Researcher* 10, no. 1 (1981): 5–10.
3. Robert K. Ream and Russell W. Rumberger, "Student Engagement, Peer Social Capital, and School Dropout Among Mexican American and Non-Latino White Students," *Sociology of Education* 81, no. 2 (2008): 109–139.
4. Nathaniel Von Der Embse, Justin Barterian, and Natasha Segool, "Test Anxiety Interventions for Children and Adolescents: A Systematic Review of Treatment Studies from 2000–2010," *Psychology in the Schools* 50, no. 1 (2013): 57–71.
5. Pew Research Center, "Mobile Fact Sheet," February 5, 2018, www.pewinternet.org/fact-sheet/mobile; Stacey A. Rutledge, Vanessa Dennen, and Lauren Bagley, "Exploring Adolescent Social Media Use in a High School: Tweeting Teens in a Bell Schedule World," *Teachers College Record* 121, no. 14 (2019): 1–37; Anna Costanza Baldry, David P. Farrington, and Anna Sorrentino, "School Bullying and Cyberbullying Among Boys and Girls: Roles and Overlap," *Journal of Aggression, Maltreatment & Trauma* 26, no. 9 (2017): 937–951; M. D. Griffiths and D. Kuss, "Adolescent Social Media Addiction (Revisited)," *Education and Health* 35, no. 3 (2017): 49–52; Lauren A. Jelenchick, Jens C. Eickhoff, and Megan A. Moreno, "'Facebook Depression'? Social Networking Site Use and Depression in Older Adolescents," *Journal of Adolescent Health* 52, no. 1 (2013): 128–130.

6. Jean M. Twenge et al., "Age, Period, and Cohort Trends in Mood Disorder Indicators and Suicide-Related Outcomes in a Nationally Representative Dataset, 2005–2017," *Journal of Abnormal Psychology* (2019).

7. Alexandra Usher and Nancy Kober, "4. What Roles Do Parent Involvement, Family Background, and Culture Play in Student Motivation?," *Center on Education Policy* (2012).

8. Valerie E. Lee, "Using Hierarchical Linear Modeling to Study Social Contexts: The Case of School Effects," *Educational psychologist* 35, no. 2 (2000): 125–141.

9. "Personalized Learning: A Working Definition," *Education Week,* October 20, 2014, www.edweek.org/ew/collections/personalized-learning-special-report-2014/a-working-definition.html.

10. Joseph A. Durlak et al., "The Impact of Enhancing Students' Social and Emotional Learning: A Meta-Analysis of School-Based Universal Interventions," *Child Development* 82, no. 1 (January 1, 2011): 405–432; J. David Hawkins et al., "Effects of Social Development Intervention in Childhood Fifteen Years Later," *Archives of Pediatrics & Adolescent Medicine* 162, no. 12 (December 2008): 1133–1141, https://doi.org/10.1001/archpedi.162.12.1133; C. Izard et al., "Emotion Knowledge as a Predictor of Social Behavior and Academic Competence in Children at Risk," *Psychological Science* 12, no. 1 (January 2001): 18–23, https://doi.org/10.1111/1467-9280.00304; Marcin Sklad et al., "Effectiveness of School-Based Universal Social, Emotional, and Behavioral Programs: Do They Enhance Students' Development in the Area of Skill, Behavior, and Adjustment?," *Psychology in the Schools* 49, no. 9 (November 2012): 892–909, https://doi.org/10.1002/pits.21641; Maurice J. Elias and Norris M. Haynes, "Social Competence, Social Support, and Academic Achievement in Minority, Low-Income, Urban Elementary School Children," *School Psychology Quarterly* 23, no. 4 (2008): 474–495, https://doi.org/10.1037/1045-3830.23.4.474; Eva Oberle et al., "Social-Emotional Competencies Make the Grade: Predicting Academic Success in Early Adolescence," *Journal of Applied Developmental Psychology* 35, no. 3 (May 1, 2014): 138–147, https://doi.org/10.1016/j.appdev.2014.02.004.

11. Oberle et al., "Social-Emotional Competencies Make the Grade."

12. Eva Oberle et al., "Establishing Systemic Social and Emotional Learning Approaches in Schools," *Cambridge Journal of Education* 46, no. 3

(July 2, 2016): 3, https://doi.org/10.1080/0305764X.2015.1125450; Elias and Haynes, "Social Competence."

13. Oberle et al., "Social-Emotional Competencies Make the Grade"; Maurice J. Elias, *Promoting Social and Emotional Learning: Guidelines for Educators* (Alexandria, VA: Association for Supervision and Curriculum, 1997); Joseph E. Zins, *Building Academic Success on Social and Emotional Learning: What Does the Research Say?* (New York: Teachers College Press, 2004).

14. Tim R. Sass and Wes Austin, "An Analysis of the Effects of Implementing Personalized Learning Connections in Broward Public Schools," working paper, September 2019, National Center on Scaling Up Effective Schools, Nashville, TN, https://my.vanderbilt.edu/scaling upcenter/files/2017/02/NCSU-PASL-early-evaluation.pdf.

15. Stacey A. Rutledge et al., "Understanding Effective High Schools: Evidence for Personalization for Academic and Social Emotional Learning," *American Educational Research Journal* 52, no. 6 (2015): 1060–1092.

16. Personalization, as discussed in this book, should not be confused with personalized learning, that is, either teacher-directed or computer-assisted instruction in which students work individually to complete courses tailored to their particular skills and knowledge.

17. Douglas C. Breunlin et al., "Personalizing a Large Comprehensive High School," *NASSP Bulletin* 89, no. 645 (2005): 24–42; Timothy J. Dyer, "Personalization: If Schools Don't Implement This One, There Will Be No Reform," *NASSP Bulletin* 80, no. 584 (1996): 1–8; Milbrey W. McLaughlin et al., "Constructing a Personalized School Environment," *Phi Delta Kappan* 72, no. 3 (1990): 230–235; Robert A. Cresswell and Patty Rasmussen, "Developing a Structure for Personalization in the High School," *NASSP Bulletin* 80, no. 584 (1996): 27–30.

18. Breunlin et al., "Personalizing a Large Comprehensive High School"; James Siddall, E. Scott Huebner, and Xu Jiang, "A Prospective Study of Differential Sources of School-Related Social Support and Adolescent Global Life Satisfaction," *American Journal of Orthopsychiatry* 83, no. 1 (2013): 107–114; Kathryn R. Wentzel et al., "Social Supports from Teachers and Peers as Predictors of Academic and Social Motivation," *Contemporary Educational Psychology* 35, no. 3 (2010): 193–202.

19. Geert Kelchtermans, "'Should I Stay or Should I Go?' Unpacking Teacher Attrition/Retention as an Educational Issue," *Teachers and Teaching* 23 , no. 8 (2017): 961–977.

20. Marisa Ann Cannata, Thomas M. Smith, and Katherine Taylor Haynes, "Integrating Academic Press and Support by Increasing Student Ownership and Responsibility," *AERA Open* 3, no. 3 (2017): 1–13, doi 10.1177/2332858417713181; Rutledge et al., "Understanding Effective High Schools."

21. Anthony S. Bryk et al., *Organizing Schools for Improvement: Lessons from Chicago* (Chicago: University of Chicago Press, 2010); Chris Dolejs, "Report on Key Practices and Policies of Consistently Higher Performing High Schools," National High School Center, 2006; Ellen Goldring et al., "Assessing Learning-Centered Leadership: Connections to Research, Professional Standards, and Current Practices," *Leadership and Policy in Schools* 8, no. 1 (2009): 1–36.

22. Jennifer L. DePaoli et al., *Building a Grad Nation: Progress and Challenge in Raising High School Graduation Rates* (Baltimore: Civic Enterprises, Everyone Graduates Center, School of Education, Johns Hopkins University, 2016), 1–91.

23. Gary Orfield and Jongyeon Ee, "Tough Choices Facing Florida's Governments: Patterns of Resegregation in Florida's Schools," LeRoy Collins Institute, Florida State University, September 27, 2017, https://civilrightsproject.ucla.edu/research/k-12-education/integration-and-diversity/patterns-of-resegregation-in-floridas-schools/LCI-Tough-Choices-Patterns-of-Resegregation_FINAL.pdf.

24. Paul G. LeMahieu et al., "Networked Improvement Communities: The Discipline of Improvement Science Meets the Power of Networks," *Quality Assurance in Education* 25, no. 1 (2017): 5–25.

25. NCSU began its multistage approach to the identification, development, and scaling of high school reform in Broward County and Fort Worth, Texas. In both districts, NCSU used value-added achievement modeling to identify the two case study districts, estimating the relative performance of the state's high schools, and then again to identify two higher and two lower performing schools within Broward County. Tim R. Sass, "Selecting High and Low-Performing High Schools in Broward County, Florida for Analysis and Treatment," Achieving Success at Scale: Research on Effective High Schools, Nashville, TN, national conference, June 2012, https://my.vanderbilt.edu/scalingupcenter/conferences/2012-conference.

26. Rutledge et al., "Understanding Effective High Schools."

27. Robert C. Pianta, "Classroom Management and Relationships Between Children and Teachers: Implications for Research and Practice,"

in *Handbook of Classroom Management*, ed. Edmund T. Emmer and Edward J. Sabornie (New York: Routledge, 2013), 695–720.

28. Stacey A. Rutledge, Lora Cohen-Vogel, and La'Tara Osborne-Lampkin, *Identifying the Characteristics of Effective High Schools: Report from Year One of the National Center on Scaling Up Effective Schools; Research Report* (National Center on Scaling Up Effective Schools, 2012).
29. Rutledge et al., "Understanding Effective High Schools,"12.
30. Goldring et al., "Assessing Learning-Centered Leadership," 1–36.
31. Rutledge et al., "Understanding Effective High Schools."
32. Rutledge et al., "*Characteristics of Effective High Schools.*
33. Albert Bandura, "Social Cognitive Theory: An Agentic Perspective," *Annual Review of Psychology* 52, no. 1 (2001): 1–26.
34. Rutledge et al., "Understanding Effective High Schools."
35. Lora Cohen-Vogel et al., "Implementing Educational Innovations at Scale: Transforming Researchers into Continuous Improvement Scientists," *Educational Policy* 29, no. 1 (2015): 257–277.
36. Rebecca Munnell McHugh et al., "Bridges and Barriers: Adolescent Perceptions of Student–Teacher Relationships," *Urban Education* 48, no. 1 (2013): 9–43.
37. Randy Isaacson and Frank Fujita, "Metacognitive Knowledge Monitoring and Self-Regulated Learning," *Journal of the Scholarship of Teaching and Learning* (2006): 39–55.
38. Kerri A. Kerr et al., "Strategies to Promote Data Use for Instructional Improvement: Actions, Outcomes, and Lessons from Three Urban Districts," *American Journal of Education* 112, no. 4 (2006): 496–520.
39. Matthew Ronfeldt et al., "Teacher Collaboration in Instructional Teams and Student Achievement," *American Educational Research Journal* 52, no. 3 (2015): 475–514.
40. Angus J. MacNeil, Doris L. Prater, and Steve Busch. "The Effects of School Culture and Climate on Student Achievement," *International Journal of Leadership in Education* 12, no. 1 (2009): 73–84.
41. Meredith I. Honig, "Complexity and Policy Implementation," in *New Directions in Education Policy Implementation: Confronting Complexity*, ed. Meredith I. Honig (Albany: State University of New York Press, 2006), 1–25.
42. Ariel Tichnor-Wagner et al., "Studying Implementation within a Continuous Continuous-Improvement Process: What Happens When We Design with Adaptations in Mind?," *Teachers College Record* 120, no. 5 (2018): n5.

43. Thomas Hatch, "What Does It Take to 'Go to Scale'? Reflections on the Promise and the Perils of Comprehensive School Reform," *Journal of Education for Students Placed at Risk* 5, no. 4 (2000): 339–354.

44. All named participants have agreed through Institutional Review Board consent to have their real names and stories shared here. Aside from those named in the book, we preserve the confidentiality of all other participants.

CHAPTER 2

1. Justine, Mrs. Tate, and Mr. Lopez are all pseudonyms.

2. Portions of this chapter are drawn from Marisa Cannata, Lora Cohen-Vogel, and Michael Sorum, "Partnering for Improvement: Communities of Practice and the Role in Scale-Up," *Peabody Journal of Education* 92, no. 5 (2017): 569–588, www.tandfonline.com/doi/full/10.1080/0 161956X.2017.1368633.

3. Sharon Feiman-Nemser, "From Preparation to Practice: Designing a Continuum to Strengthen and Sustain Teaching," *Teachers College Record* 103, no. 6 (2001): 1013–1055.

4. Barry J. Fishman et al., "Design-Based Implementation Research: An Emerging Model for Transforming the Relationship of Research and Practice," in *Design-Based Implementation Research: Theories, Methods, and Exemplars*, ed. Barry J. Fishman et al. (New York: Teachers College, Columbia University, 2013), 136–156.

5. Mark Berends, Susan Bodilly, and Sheila Nataraj Kirby, *Facing the Challenges of Whole-School Reform: New American Schools After a Decade*, MR-1498-EDU (Santa Monica, CA: Rand, 2002), www.rand .org/pubs/research_briefs/RB8019/index1.html; Amanda Datnow, Lea Hubbard, and Hugh Mehan, *Extending Educational Reform: From One School to Many* (New York: Routledge, 2002); Thomas K. Glennan et al., *Expanding the Reach of Education Reforms: Perspectives from Leaders in the Scale-Up of Educational Interventions* (New York: Rand, 2004).

6. Anthony S. Bryk et al., *Learning to Improve: How America's Schools Can Get Better at Getting Better* (Cambridge, MA: Harvard Education Press, 2015); Lora Cohen-Vogel et al., "Implementing Educational Innovations at Scale: Transforming Researchers Into Continuous Improvement Scientists," *Educational Policy* 29, no. 1 (2015): 257–277.

7. Bryk et al., *Learning to Improve*; Anthony S. Bryk, Louis Gomez and Alicia Grunow, "Getting Ideas into Action: Building Networked Improvement Communities in Education," in *Frontiers in Sociology*

of Education, ed. Maureen T. Hallinan (New York: Springer, 2011), 127–162.

8. Leah Teeters, "Conceptualizing Research Practice Partnerships as Joint Work," National Center for Research in Policy and Practice, May 14, 2015, http://ncrpp.org/blog/2015/conceptualizing-research-practice -partnerships-as-joint-work.

9. Amanda Datnow and Vicki Park, "Conceptualizing Policy Implementation: Large-Scale Reform in an Era of Complexity," in *Handbook of Education Policy Research*, ed. Gary Sykes, Barbara Schneider, and David N. Plank (New York: Routledge, 2009), 348–361; Milbrey W. McLaughlin, "Implementation as Mutual Adaptation: Change in Classroom Organization," *Teachers College Record* 7 (February 1976): 339–351; Leslie Santee Siskin, "Mutual Adaptation in Action," *Teachers College Record* 118, no. 13 (2016): 1–18.

10. Cannata and Rutledge, "New Frontiers in Scaling Up Research."

11. Maggie Hannan et al., "Using Improvement Science to Better Support Beginning Teachers: The Case of the Building a Teaching Effectiveness Network," *Journal of Teacher Education* 66, no. 5 (2015): 494–508, https://doi.org/10.1177/0022487115602126.

12. Bryk, Gomez, and Grunow, "Getting Ideas into Action"; Jennifer Lin Russell et al., "A Framework for the Initiation of Networked Improvement Communities," *Teachers College Record* 119, no. 7 (2017): 1–36.

13. Paul G. LeMahieu et al., "Networked Improvement Communities: The Discipline of Improvement Science Meets the Power of Networks," *Quality Assurance in Education* 25, no. 1 (January 6, 2017): 5–25, https://doi.org/10.1108/QAE-12-2016-0084.

14. Douglas C. Engelbart, "Toward High-Performance Organizations: A Strategic Role for Groupware," Bootstrap Institute, San Jose, CA, June 1992, www.dougengelbart.org/pubs/augment-132811.html#3.

15. LeMahieu et al., "Networked Improvement Communities."

16. Bryk, Gomez, and Grunow, "Getting Ideas into Action"; Laura D'Amico, "The Center for Learning Technologies in Urban Schools: Evolving Relationships in Design-Based Research," in *Research and Practice in Education: Building Alliances, Bridging the Divide*, ed. Cynthia E. Coburn and Mary Kay Stein (Lanham, MD: Rowman & Littlefield, 2010), 37–54.

17. Bryk, Gomez, and Grunow, "Getting Ideas into Action," 5.

18. David A. Chambers, Russell E. Glasgow, and Kurt C. Stange, "The Dynamic Sustainability Framework: Addressing the Paradox of

Sustainment amid Ongoing Change," *Implementation Science* 8 (2013): 117.

19. Bryk, Gomez, and Grunow, "Getting Ideas into Action."

20. Bryk, Gomez, and Grunow, "Getting Ideas into Action."

21. Bryk et al., *Learning to Improve.*

22. Nicole Sowers and Hiroyuki Yamada, "Community College Pathways: 2013–2014 Descriptive Report," Carnegie Foundation for the Advancement of Teaching, Stanford, CA, January 2015, https://eric.ed .gov/?id=ED554591.

23. Cynthia E. Coburn, "Rethinking Scale: Moving Beyond Numbers to Deep and Lasting Change," *Educational Researcher* 32, no. 6 (August 1, 2003): 3–12, https://doi.org/10.3102/0013189X032006003.

24. Russell et al., "Networked Improvement Communities"; Lora Cohen-Vogel et al., "A Model of Continuous Improvement in High Schools: A Process for Research, Innovation Design, Implementation, and Scale," *Teachers College Record* 116, no. 13 (2016); Marisa Cannata, Chris Redding, and Tuan Nguyen, "Building Student Ownership and Responsibility: Examining Student Outcomes from a Research-Practice Partnership," *Journal of Research on Educational Effectiveness* 12, no. 3 (2019): 333–362.

25. Richard Elmore, "Getting to Scale with Good Educational Practice," *Harvard Educational Review* 66, no. 1 (April 1, 1996): 1–27; Jonathan A Supovitz, *The Case for District-Based Reform: Leading, Building, and Sustaining School Improvement* (Cambridge, MA: Harvard Education Press, 2006); James P. Spillane, Brian J. Reiser, and Todd Reimer, "Policy Implementation and Cognition: Reframing and Refocusing Implementation Research," *Review of Educational Research* 72, no. 3 (September 1, 2002): 387–431, https://doi.org/10.3102/0034654 3072003387.

26. Cohen-Vogel et al., "Implementing Educational Innovations at Scale."

27. Cannata, Cohen-Vogel, and Sorum, "Partnering for Improvement"; LeMahieu et al., "Networked Improvement Communities"; Datnow and Park, "Conceptualizing Policy Implementation"; Siskin, "Mutual Adaptation in Action."

28. Chris Redding and Samantha Viano, "Co-Creating School Reform: Should Self-Determination Be a Component of School Improvement?," *Teachers College Record* 120, no. 11 (2018).

29. Chris Redding, Marisa Cannata, and Jason Miller, "System Learning in an Urban School District: A Case Study of Intra-District Learning," *Journal of Educational Change* 19, no. 1 (2018): 77–101; Russell et al., "Networked Improvement Communities."

30. Cannata, Cohen-Vogel, and Sorum, "Partnering for Improvement."
31. Cheryl King et al., "Designing Innovations for Implementation at Scale: An Emerging Framework for Increasing System Capacity," Achieving Success at Scale: Research on Effective High Schools, Nashville, TN, national conference, June 2012, https://my.vanderbilt.edu /scalingupcenter/conferences/2012-conference.
32. Lora Cohen-Vogel et al., "Organizing for School Improvement: The Dilemmas of Research-Practice Partnerships," *Journal of Research on Organization in Education* 2, no. 1 (2018): 1–24.
33. Russell et al., "Networked Improvement Communities."
34. Camille A. Farrington et al., "Teaching Adolescents to Become Learners: The Role of Noncognitive Factors in Shaping School Performance—A Critical Literature Review," University of Chicago Consortium on Chicago School Research, 2012; Joseph F. Murphy, "The Evolution of the High School in America," *Teachers College Record* 116, no. 13 (2016): 1–18.
35. Eva Oberle et al., "Establishing Systemic Social and Emotional Learning Approaches in Schools: A Framework for Schoolwide Implementation," *Cambridge Journal of Education* 46, no. 3 (July 2, 2016): 3, https://doi.org/10.1080/0305764X.2015.1125450.
36. J. David Hawkins et al., "Effects of Social Development Intervention in Childhood Fifteen Years Later," *Archives of Pediatrics & Adolescent Medicine* 162, no. 12 (December 2008): 1133–1141, https://doi.org /10.1001/archpedi.162.12.1133.
37. King et al., "Designing Innovations for Implementation at Scale."
38. Russell et al., "Networked Improvement Communities."
39. Jennifer A. Fredricks, "Extracurricular Participation and Academic Outcomes: Testing the Over-Scheduling Hypothesis," *Journal of Youth and Adolescence* 41, no. 3 (March 1, 2012): 295–306, https://doi.org /10.1007/s10964-011-9704-0; Ralph B. McNeal, "Extracurricular Activities and High School Dropouts," *Sociology of Education* 68, no. 1 (1995): 62–81.
40. Ariel Tichnor-Wagner et al., "Continuous Improvement in the Public School Context: Understanding How Educators Respond to Plan-Do-Study-Act Cycles," *Journal of Educational Change* 18, no. 4 (2017): 465–94.
41. Tichnor-Wagner et al., "How Educators Respond to Plan-Do-Study-Act Cycles."
42. Stacey A. Rutledge et al., "Exploring the Promise of Continuous Improvement Strategies within the Bureaucratic Structure of American

High Schools," presentation at annual meeting of the American Educational Research Association, San Antonio, TX, 2017.

43. Engelbart, "Strategic Role for Groupware."

44. Bryk et al., *Learning to Improve.*

45. Tichnor-Wagner et al., "How Educators Respond to Plan-Do-Study-Act Cycles."

46. Russell et al., "Networked Improvement Communities."

47. Russell et al., "Networked Improvement Communities."

48. Redding, Cannata, and Miller, "A Case Study of Intra-District Learning."

CHAPTER 3

1. Ms. Cornelius and Ms. Martinez are pseudonyms.

2. Ms. Green is a pseudonym.

3. Heather P. Libbey, "Measuring Student Relationships to School: Attachment, Bonding, Connectedness, and Engagement," *Journal of school health* 74, no. 7 (2004): 274–283.

4. Joseph A. Durlak et al., "The Impact of Enhancing Students' Social and Emotional Learning: A Meta-Analysis of School-Based Universal Interventions," *Child Development* 82, no. 1 (2011): 405–432; Jacquelynne S. Eccles et al., "The Relation of Connection, Regulation, and Support for Autonomy to Adolescents' Functioning," *Journal of Adolescent Research* 12, no. 2 (1997): 263–286.

5. Kyle M. McCallumore and Ervin F. Sparapani, "The Importance of the Ninth Grade on High School Graduation Rates and Student Success in High School," *Education* 130, no. 3 (2010): 447–456; Penelope J. Fritzer and Paula S. Herbst, "'Make Yourself at Home': The 'House' Concept in Ninth Grade Transition," *American Secondary Education* 25, no. 2 (1996): 7–9; Hanna Melnick, Channa M. Cook-Harvey, and Linda Darling-Hammond, "Encouraging Social and Emotional Learning in the Context of New Accountability," Learning Policy Institute, April 2017, https://learningpolicyinstitute.org/sites/default/files/product-files/Social_Emotional_Learning_New_Accountability_REPORT.pdf.

6. Na'ilah Suad Nasir, Amina Jones, and Milbrey W. McLaughlin, "School Connectedness for Students in Low-Income Urban High Schools," *Teachers College Record* (2011).

7. Camille A. Farrington et al., "Teaching Adolescents to Become Learners: The Role of Noncognitive Factors in Shaping School Performance; A Critical Literature Review," University of Chicago Consortium on Chicago School Research, June 2012.

8. Rebecca Munnell McHugh et al., "Bridges and Barriers: Adolescent Perceptions of Student–Teacher Relationships," *Urban Education* 48, no. 1 (2013): 9–43.

9. McHugh et al., "Bridges and Barriers," 19.

10. Ann S. Masten and Marie-Gabrielle J. Reed, "Resilience in Development," in *Handbook of Positive Psychology*, ed. Shane J. Lopez et al. (Oxford: Oxford University Press, 2002), 74–88.

11. Albert Bandura, "Self-Efficacy: Toward a Unifying Theory of Behavioral Change," *Psychological Review* 84, no. 2 (1977): 191; Albert Bandura, "Social Cognitive Theory: An Agentic Perspective," *Annual Review of Psychology* 52 (2001): 1–26; Barry J. Zimmerman, "Self-Efficacy: An Essential Motive to Learn," *Contemporary Educational Psychology* 25, no. 1 (2000): 82–91.

12. James P. Connell and James G. Wellborn, "Competence, Autonomy, and Relatedness: A Motivational Analysis of Self-System Processes," in *Minnesota Symposia on Child Psychology*, vol. 23, *Self-Processes and Development*, ed. M. R. Gunnar et al. (Hillsdale, NJ: Lawrence Erlbaum Associates, 1991), 43–77.

13. Ji Y. Hong, "Why Do Some Beginning Teachers Leave the School, and Others Stay? Understanding Teacher Resilience Through Psychological Lenses," *Teachers and Teaching* 18, no. 4 (2012): 417–440.

14. McHugh et al., "Bridges and Barriers," 9–43; Brian C. Patrick, Jennifer Hisley, and Toni Kempler, "'What's Everybody So Excited About?': The Effects of Teacher Enthusiasm on Student Intrinsic Motivation and Vitality," *Journal of Experimental Education* 68, no. 3 (2000): 217–236.

15. Sonia Nieto, *The Light in Their Eyes: Creating Multicultural Learning Communities* (New York: Teachers College Press, 2015).

16. Becky A. Smerdon, "Students' Perceptions of Membership in Their High Schools," *Sociology of Education* 75, no. 4 (2002): 297.

17. Vincent A. Anfara, "Advisor–Advisee Programs: Important but Problematic," *Middle School Journal* 38, no. 1 (2006): 54–60.

18. John P. Galassi, Suzanne A. Gulledge, and Nancy D. Cox, "Middle School Advisories: Retrospect and Prospect," *Review of Educational Research* 67, no. 3 (1997): 301–338.

19. Douglas Mac Iver, "Meeting the Needs of Young Adolescents: Advisory Groups, Interdisciplinary Teaching Teams, and School Transition Programs," *Phi Delta Kappan* 71, no. 6 (1990): 458–464.

20. Paul S. George and Lynn Oldaker, *Evidence for the Middle School* (Columbus, OH: National Middle School Association, 1985).

21. Institute of Education Sciences, "Check & Connect: Dropout Prevention," What Works Clearinghouse, last updated May 2015, https://ies .ed.gov/ncee/wwc/EvidenceSnapshot/78.

22. Mary F. Sinclair et al., "Facilitating Student Engagement: Lessons Learned from Check & Connect Longitudinal Studies," *California School Psychologist* 8, no. 1 (2003): 34.

23. Brandy R. Maynard, Elizabeth K. Kjellstrand, and Aaron M. Thompson, "Effects of Check and Connect on Attendance, Behavior, and Academics: A Randomized Effectiveness Trial," *Research on Social Work Practice* 24, no. 3 (2014): 296–309.

24. Katie Wolfe et al., "A Systematic Review of the Empirical Support for Check-In Check-Out," *Journal of Positive Behavior Interventions* 18, no. 2 (2016): 74–88, doi: 10.1177/1098300715595957.

25. Daniel M. Maggin et al., "A Systematic Evidence Review of the Check-In/Check-Out Program for Reducing Student Challenging Behaviors," *Journal of Positive Behavior Interventions* 17, no. 4 (2015): 197–208.

26. Anfara, "Advisor–Advisee Programs," 54–60.

CHAPTER 4

1. Student names are pseudonyms.

2. Randy M. Isaacson and Frank Fujita, "Metacognitive Knowledge Monitoring and Self-Regulated Learning: Academic Success and Reflections on Learning," *Journal of Scholarship of Teaching and Learning* 6, no. 1 (August 2006): 39–55; Gary P. Latham and Edwin A. Locke, "New Developments in and Directions for Goal-Setting Research," *European Psychologist* 12, no. 4 (2007): 290–300; Aleidine J. Moeller, Janine M. Theiler, and Chaorong Wu, "Goal Setting and Student Achievement: A Longitudinal Study," *Modern Language Journal* 96, no. 2 (2012): 153–169; Barry J. Zimmerman, "Self-Regulated Learning and Academic Achievement: An Overview," *Educational Psychologist* 25, no. 1 (1990): 3–17; Edwin A. Locke and Gary P. Latham, "New Directions in Goal-Setting Theory," *Current Directions in Psychological Science* 15, no. 5 (October 1, 2006): 265–268, https://doi.org/10.1111/j.1467-8721.2006.00449.x; Felissa K. Lee, Kennon M. Sheldon, and Daniel B. Turban, "Personality and the Goal-Striving Process: The Influence of Achievement Goal Patterns, Goal Level, and Mental Focus on Performance and Enjoyment," *Journal of Applied Psychology* 88, no. 2 (2003): 256–265, https://doi.org/10.1037/0021-9010.88.2.256.

3. Collaborative for Academic, Social, and Emotional Learning (CA-SEL), "Effective Social and Emotional Learning Programs: Middle and High School Edition," CASEL, Chicago, 2015, http://secondaryguide.casel.org/casel-secondary-guide.pdf.

4. Barry J. Zimmerman and Dale H. Schunk, "Motivation: An Essential Dimension of Self-Regulated Learning," in *Motivation and Self-Regulated Learning: Theory, Research, and Applications*, ed. Dale H. Schunk and Barry J. Zimmerman (New York: Lawrence Erlbaum Associates, 2008), 1; Camille Farrington et al., "Teaching Adolescents to Become Learners: The Role of Noncognitive Factors in Shaping School Performance—A Critical Literature Review," University of Chicago Consortium on Chicago School Research, 2012.

5. Silke Weisweiler et al., "Gaining Insight to Transfer of Training through the Lens of Social Psychology," *Educational Research Review*, Special Issue: Transfer of Training: New Conceptualizations Through Integrated Research Perspectives, 8 (January 1, 2013): 14–27, https://doi.org/10.1016/j.edurev.2012.05.006. See also Andrew J. Elliot and James W. Fryer, "The Goal Construct in Psychology," *Handbook of Motivation Science* 18 (2008): 235–250; Zimmerman and Schunk, "Motivation: An Essential Dimension"; Johnmarshall Reeve and Woogul Lee, "Students' Classroom Engagement Produces Longitudinal Changes in Classroom Motivation," *Journal of Educational Psychology* 106, no. 2 (2014): 527; Dale Schunk, "Self-Efficacy for Reading and Writing: Influence of Modeling, Goal Setting, and Self-Evaluation," *Reading & Writing Quarterly* 19 (January 1, 2003): 159–172; Sylvia D. Kreibig, Guido H. E. Gendolla, and Klaus R. Scherer, "Psychophysiological Effects of Emotional Responding to Goal Attainment," *Biological Psychology* 84, no. 3 (2010): 474–487; Locke and Latham, "Goal-Setting Theory"; Andrew Macleod, Emma Coates, and Jacquie Hetherton, "Increasing Well-Being Through Teaching Goal-Setting and Planning Skills: Results of a Brief Intervention," *Journal of Happiness Studies* 9 (February 1, 2008): 185–196, https://doi.org/10.1007/s10902-007-9057-2; Annemaree Carroll et al., "Goal Setting and Self-Efficacy Among Delinquent, At-Risk and Not At-Risk Adolescents," *Journal of Youth and Adolescence* 42, no. 3 (March 1, 2013): 431–443, https://doi.org/10.1007/s10964-012-9799-y.

6. Moeller, Theiler, and Wu, "Goal Setting and Student Achievement." See also Kenneth E. Barron and Judith M. Harackiewicz, "Achievement Goals and Optimal Motivation: Testing Multiple Goal Models," *Journal of Personality and Social Psychology* 80, no. 5 (2001): 706.

7. Chi-Cheng Chang et al., "Using E-Portfolio for Learning Goal Setting to Facilitate Self-Regulated Learning of High School Students," *Behaviour & Information Technology* 37, no. 12 (August 1, 2018): 1237–1251, https://doi.org/10.1080/0144929X.2018.1496275. See also Angela Duckworth et al., "From Fantasy to Action: Mental Contrasting With Implementation Intentions (MCII) Improves Academic Performance in Children," *Social Psychological and Personality Science* 4 (October 14, 2013), https://doi.org/10.1177/1948550613476307; Farrington et al., "Teaching Adolescents to Become Learners"; Lisa S. Blackwell, Kali H. Trzesniewski, and Carol Sorich Dweck, "Implicit Theories of Intelligence Predict Achievement Across an Adolescent Transition: A Longitudinal Study and an Intervention," *Child Development* 78, no. 1 (January 1, 2007): 246–263, https://doi.org /10.1111/j.1467-8624.2007.00995.x; Valerie L. Mazzotti, David W. Test, and Charles L. Wood, "Effects of Multimedia Goal-Setting Instruction on Students' Knowledge of the Self-Determined Learning Model of Instruction and Disruptive Behavior," *Journal of Positive Behavior Interventions* 15, no. 2 (April 1, 2013): 90–102, https://doi .org/10.1177/1098300712440452.

8. Locke and Latham, "Goal-Setting Theory,"

9. Locke and Latham, "Goal-Setting Theory"; Lee, Sheldon, and Turban, "Personality and the Goal-Striving Process."

10. M. V. Covington, "Goal Theory, Motivation, and School Achievement: An Integrative Review," *Annual Review of Psychology* 51 (2000): 171–200, https://doi.org/10.1146/annurev.psych.51.1.171.

11. Covington, "Goal Theory," 174.

12. Kati Vasalampi et al., "The Role of Goal-Related Autonomous Motivation, Effort and Progress in the Transition to University," *European Journal of Psychology of Education* 27, no. 4 (December 1, 2012): 591–604, https://doi.org/10.1007/s10212-011-0098-x.

13. Reeve and Lee, "Students' Classroom Engagement."

14. Carol S. Dweck and Allison Master, "Self-Theories Motivate Self-Regulated Learning," in *Motivation and Self-Regulated Learning: Theory, Research, and Applications*, ed. Dale H. Schunk and Barry J. Zimmerman (New York: Lawrence Erlbaum Associates, 2008), 31–52; Barron and Harackiewicz, "Achievement Goals and Optimal Motivation."

15. Gerard H. Seijts and Gary P. Latham, "Learning Versus Performance Goals: When Should Each Be Used?," *Academy of Management Executive (1993–2005)* 19, no. 1 (2005): 128.

16. Covington, "Goal Theory"; Gerard H. Seijts and Gary P. Latham, "Learning Versus Performance Goals: When Should Each Be Used?," *Academy of Management Executive (1993–2005)* 19, no. 1 (2005): 124–131; Schunk, "Self-Efficacy for Reading and Writing"; Zimmerman and Schunk, "Motivation: An Essential Dimension"; Locke and Latham, "Goal-Setting Theory"; Lee, Sheldon, and Turban, "Personality and the Goal-Striving Process"; Karen Weber Cullen, Tom Baranowski, and Stella P. Smith, "Using Goal Setting as a Strategy for Dietary Behavior Change," *Journal of the American Dietetic Association* 101, no. 5 (May 1, 2001): 562–566, https://doi.org/10.1016/S0002-8223(01)00140-7; Brian R. Belland, ChanMin Kim, and Michael J. Hannafin, "A Framework for Designing Scaffolds That Improve Motivation and Cognition," *Educational Psychologist* 48, no. 4 (October 1, 2013): 243–270, https://doi.org/10.1080/00461520.2013.838920.

17. Gabriele Oettingen and Julie Y. A. Cachia, "Problems with Positive Thinking and How to Overcome Them," in *Handbook of Self-Regulation: Research, Theory, and Applications*, 3rd ed., ed. K. D. Vohs and R. F. Baumeister (New York: Guilford Press, 2016), 547–570; Angela Lee Duckworth et al., "Self-Regulation Strategies Improve Self-Discipline in Adolescents: Benefits of Mental Contrasting and Implementation Intentions," *Educational Psychology* 31, no. 1 (2011): 17–26.

18. Oettingen and Cachia, "Problems with Positive Thinking."

19. A. Kappes and Gabriele Oettingen, "The Emergence of Goal Pursuit: Mental Contrasting Connects Future and Reality," *Journal of Experimental Social Psychology* 54 (2014): 25–39.

20. Oettingen and Cachia, "Problems with Positive Thinking," 555.

21. Weisweiler et al., "Transfer of Training through the Lens of Social Psychology," 18.

22. Peter M. Gollwitzer, "Implementation Intentions: Strong Effects of Simple Plans," *American Psychologist* 54, no. 7 (1999): 493–503, https://doi.org/10.1037/0003-066X.54.7.493.

23. Duckworth et al., "From Fantasy to Action."

24. Duckworth et al., "Self-Regulation Strategies."

25. See the following sources on goal setting and self-regulation: Mazzotti, Test, and Wood, "Multimedia Goal-Setting Instruction"; Timothy J. Cleary and Barry J. Zimmerman, "Self-Regulation Empowerment Program: A School-Based Program to Enhance Self-Regulated and Self-Motivated Cycles of Student Learning," *Psychology in the Schools* 41, no. 5 (May 2004): 537–550, https://doi.org/10.1002/pits.10177; Barry J. Zimmerman, "Goal-Setting: A Key Proactive Source of Academic

Self-Regulation," in *Motivation and Self-Regulated Learning: Theory, Research, and Applications*, ed. Dale H. Schunk and Barry J. Zimmerman (New York: Lawrence Erlbaum Associates, 2008), 267–229; Moeller, Theiler, and Wu, "Goal Setting and Student Achievement"; Cullen, Baranowski, and Smith, "Strategy for Dietary Behavior Change."

26. Zimmerman and Schunk, "Motivation: An Essential Dimension," 1.

27. Belland, Kim, and Hannafin, "Scaffolds That Improve Motivation and Cognition"; Latham and Locke, "Directions for Goal-Setting Research"; Zimmerman, "Goal-Setting: A Key Proactive Source."

28. Belland, Kim, and Hannafin, "Scaffolds That Improve Motivation and Cognition"; Latham and Locke, "Directions for Goal-Setting Research"; Zimmerman, "Goal-Setting: A Key Proactive Source."

29. Belland, Kim, and Hannafin, "Scaffolds That Improve Motivation and Cognition."

30. Locke and Latham, "Goal-Setting Theory"; Christopher H. Utman and Stephen G. Harkins, "The Effect of Increasing Ego Involvement on the Potency of the Potential for Self-Evaluation," *Journal of Applied Social Psychology* 40, no. 7 (July 1, 2010): 1579–1604, https://doi.org/10.1111/j.1559-1816.2010.00630.x; Cullen, Baranowski, and Smith, "Strategy for Dietary Behavior Change."

31. Chang et al., "E-Portfolio for Learning Goal Setting."

32. Schunk, "Self-Efficacy for Reading and Writing,"

33. Kreibig, Gendolla, and Scherer, "Psychophysiological Effects."

34. Locke and Latham, "New Directions in Goal-Setting Theory"; Utman and Harkins, "Increasing Ego Involvement"; Cullen, Baranowski, and Smith, "Strategy for Dietary Behavior Change"; Chang et al., "E-Portfolio for Learning Goal Setting."

35. Cynthia E. Coburn, "Rethinking Scale: Moving Beyond Numbers to Deep and Lasting Change," *Educational Researcher* 32, no. 6 (August 1, 2003): 3–12, https://doi.org/10.3102/0013189X032006003.

36. Amanda Datnow Coburn, Lea Hubbard, and Hugh Mehan, *Extending Educational Reform: From One School to Many* (New York: Routledge, 2002).

37. Lora Cohen-Vogel et al., "A Model of Continuous Improvement in High Schools: A Process for Research, Innovation Design, Implementation, and Scale," *Teachers College Record* 116, no. 13 (2016): 1–26.

38. Maggie Hannan et al., "Using Improvement Science to Better Support Beginning Teachers: The Case of the Building a Teaching Effectiveness

Network," *Journal of Teacher Education* 66, no. 5 (2015): 494–508, https://doi.org/10.1177/0022487115602126.

39. Coburn, "Rethinking Scale."

40. Sandra A. Deemer, "Classroom Goal Orientation in High School Classrooms: Revealing Links Between Teacher Beliefs and Classroom Environments," *Educational Research* 46, no. 1 (2004): 73–90; Covington, "Goal Theory."

CHAPTER 5

1. "Behavioral and Academic Support Information System (BASIS)," Broward County Public Schools, accessed September 24, 2019, www .browardschools.com/Page/32943.

2. Participants at one of the lower performing schools believed that the use of data led to greater accountability and scrutiny over their performance.

3. Stacey A. Rutledge et al., "Understanding Effective High Schools: Evidence for Personalization for Academic and Social Emotional Learning," *American Educational Research Journal* 52, no. 6 (2015): 1074.

4. Thomas Hatch, "What Does It Take to "Go to Scale"? Reflections on the Promise and the Perils of Comprehensive School Reform," *Journal of Education for Students Placed at Risk* 5, no. 4 (2000): 339–354.

5. Kerri A. Kerr et al., "Strategies to Promote Data Use for Instructional Improvement: Actions, Outcomes, and Lessons from Three Urban Districts," *American Journal of Education* 112, no. 4 (2006): 496–520; Amanda Datnow, Vicki Park, and Brianna Kennedy-Lewis, "High School Teachers' Use of Data to Inform Instruction," *Journal of Education for Students Placed at Risk* 17, no. 4 (2012): 247–265.

6. Julie Marsh and Caitlin C. Farrell, "How Leaders Can Support Teachers with Data-Driven Decision Making: A Framework for Understanding Capacity Building," *Educational Management Administration & Leadership* 43, no. 2 (2015): 269–289; Elizabeth Farley-Ripple and Joan Buttram, "The Development of Capacity for Data Use: The Role of Teacher Networks in an Elementary School," *Teachers College Record* 117, no. 4 (2015): 1–34; Laura Hamilton et al., "Using Student Achievement Data to Support Instructional Decision Making," US Department of Education, September 2009, https://ies.ed.gov/ncee /wwc/Docs/PracticeGuide/dddm_pg_092909.pdf; Eva Oberle et al., "Establishing Systemic Social and Emotional Learning Approaches in

Schools: A Framework for Schoolwide Implementation," *Cambridge Journal of Education* 46, no. 3 (2016): 277–297.

7. Alex Bowers, "What's in a Grade? The Multidimensional Nature of What Teacher-Assigned Grades Assess in High School," *Educational Research and Evaluation* 17, no. 3 (2011): 141–159.

8. Lora Cohen-Vogel and Christopher Harrison, "Leading with Data: Evidence from the National Center on Scaling Up Effective Schools," *Leadership and Policy in Schools* 12, no. 2 (2013): 122–145.

9. To be sure, there are cons with using data in schools. Student data is used in public schools as a tool for course placement. When the data is used poorly, students might be placed in academic courses that are not the most appropriate for them. With access to information on a student's prior behavior, teachers and administrators might make assumptions about a student, rather than giving the teen a clean slate.

10. Dorothea Anagnostopoulos, Stacey A. Rutledge, and Rebecca Jacobsen, "Mapping the Information Infrastructure of Accountability," in *The Infrastructure of Accountability: Data Use and the Transformation of American Education*, ed. Dorothea Anagnostopoulos, Stacey A. Rutledge, and Rebecca Jacobsen (Cambridge, MA: Harvard Education Press, 2013), 1–20.

11. Mei Kuin Lai and Kim Schildkamp, "Data-Based Decision Making: An Overview," In *Data-Based Decision Making in Education: Challenges and Opportunities*, ed. Kim Schildkamp, Mei Kuin Lai, and Lorna Earl (New York: Springer, 2013), 9–21; Stephen Anderson, Kenneth Leithwood, and Tiiu Strauss, "Leading Data Use in Schools: Organizational Conditions and Practices at the School and District Levels," *Leadership and Policy in Schools* 9, no. 3 (2010): 292–327; Richard Halverson et al., "The New Instructional Leadership: Creating Data-Driven Instructional Systems in School," *Journal of School Leadership* 17, no. 2 (2007): 159–194.

12. Leyton Schnellert, Deborah Butler, and Stephanie Higginson, "Co-Constructors of Data, Co-Constructors of Meaning: Teacher Professional Development in an Age of Accountability," *Teaching and Teacher Education* 24, no. 3 (2008): 725–750.

13. Marsh and Farrell, "How Leaders Can Support Teachers," 269–289. See also Jo Beth Jimerson and Jeffrey Wayman, "Professional Learning for Using Data: Examining Teacher Needs and Supports," *Teachers College Record* 117, no. 4 (2015): n4; Farley-Ripple and Buttram, "Teacher Networks in an Elementary School," 1–34.

14. Nancy Gerzon, "Structuring Professional Learning to Develop a Culture of Data Use: Aligning Knowledge from the Field and Research Findings," *Teachers College Record* 117, no. 4 (2015): n4; Jeffrey Wayman, "Involving Teachers in Data-Driven Decision Making: Using Computer Data Systems to Support Teacher Inquiry and Reflection," *Journal of Education for Students Placed at Risk* 10, no. 3 (2005): 295–308; Viki Young, "Teachers' Use of Data: Loose Coupling, Agenda Setting, and Team Norms," *American Journal of Education* 112, no. 4 (2006): 521–548.

15. Marsh and Farrell, "How Leaders Can Support Teachers," 269–289.

16. Anagnostopoulos, Rutledge, and Jacobsen, "Information Infrastructure of Accountability," 1–20; Lawrence Gallagher, Barbara Means, and Christine Padilla, "Teachers' Use of Student Data Systems to Improve Instruction: 2005 to 2007," US Department of Education, 2008; Priscilla Wohlstetter, Amanda Datnow, and Vicki Park, "Creating a System for Data-Driven Decision-Making: Applying the Principal-Agent Framework," *School Effectiveness and School Improvement* 19, no. 3 (2008): 239–259; Halverson et al., "New Instructional Leadership," 159–194; Kerr et. al., Strategies to Promote Data Use," 496–520; Richard Murnane, Nancy Sharkey, and Kathryn Boudett, "Using Student-Assessment Results to Improve Instruction: Lessons from a Workshop," *Journal of Education for Students Placed At Risk* 10, no. 3 (2005): 269–280.

17. Jonathan Supovitz, "Knowledge-Based Organizational Learning for Instructional Improvement," in *Second International Handbook of Educational Change*, ed. Andy Hargreaves et al. (New York: Springer, 2010), 707–723.

18. Supovitz, "Knowledge-Based Organizational Learning," 707–723; Rutledge et al., "Understanding Effective High Schools," 1074.

CHAPTER 6

1. The PASL program at Blanche Ely High School described here focuses on the first two years of implementation. During those years, the school placed great emphasis on implementing PASL. The school's adherence to the reform declined in subsequent years, when leadership at the school changed. We address this challenge in the final chapter of this book.

2. Anit Somech and Anat Drach-Zahavy, "Schools as Team-Based Organizations: A Structure-Process-Outcomes Approach," *Group Dynamics: Theory, Research, and Practice* 11, no. 4 (2007): 305.

3. Leslie Santee Siskin and Judith Warren Little, "The Subject Department: Continuities and Critiques," in *The Subjects in Question: Departmental Organization and the High School,* ed. Leslie Santee Siskin and Judith Warren Little (New York: Teachers College Press, 1995), 32–49.

4. Matthew Ronfeldt et al., "Teacher Collaboration in Instructional Teams and Student Achievement," *American Educational Research Journal* 52, no. 3 (2015): 475–514; Vicki Vescio, Dorene Ross, and Alyson Adams, "A Review of Research on the Impact of Professional Learning Communities on Teaching Practice and Student Learning," *Teaching and Teacher Education* 24, no. 1 (2008): 80–91.

5. Min Sun, Susanna Loeb, and Jason A. Grissom, "Building Teacher Teams: Evidence of Positive Spillovers from More Effective Colleagues," *Educational Evaluation and Policy Analysis* 39, no. 1 (2017): 104–125.

6. Robert D. Felner et al., "Creating Small Learning Communities: Lessons from the Project on High-Performing Learning Communities About 'What Works' in Creating Productive, Developmentally Enhancing, Learning Contexts," *Educational Psychologist* 42, no. 4 (2007): 209–221. See also Diana Oxley, "Organizing Schools into Small Learning Communities," *National Association of Secondary School Principals Bulletin* 85, no. 625 (2001): 5; Jonathan A. Supovitz and Jolley B. Christman, "Small Learning Communities That Actually Learn: Lessons for School Leaders," *Phi Delta Kappan* 86, no. 9 (2005): 649–651.

7. Felner et al., "Creating Small Learning Communities."

8. Richard DuFour and Rebecca DuFour, *Learning by Doing: A Handbook for Professional Learning Communities at Work* (Bloomington, IN: Solution Tree Press, 2013); Vescio, Ross, and Adams, "Impact of Professional Learning."

9. Vescio, Ross, and Adams, "Impact of Professional Learning Communities," 89.

10. Yvonne L. Goddard, Roger D. Goddard, and Megan Tschannen-Moran, "A Theoretical and Empirical Investigation of Teacher Collaboration for School Improvement and Student Achievement in Public Elementary Schools," *Teachers College Record* 109, no. 4 (2007): 877–896; Seth A. King, Christopher J. Lemons, and David R. Hill, "Response to Intervention in Secondary Schools: Considerations for Administrators," *National Association of Secondary School Principals Bulletin* 96, no. 1 (2012): 5–22.

11. Selçuk Doğan, Rose Pringle, and Jennifer Mesa, "The Impacts of Professional Learning Communities on Science Teachers' Knowledge, Practice and Student Learning: A Review," *Professional Development in Education* 42, no. 4 (2016): 569–588.

12. Daniel L. Burke, "Looping: Adding Time, Strengthening Relationships; ERIC Digest," Educational Resources Information Center, 1997; Justina D. Pedante, "The Effects of School Counselor Looping from Middle to High School on the Experience of Transition for Students" (PhD diss., Immaculata College, 2006); Robert A. Ovalle, "Why Isn't Looping a More Common Practice? A Leadership Case Study," *International Journal of Educational Reform* 13, no. 2 (2004): 136–142.

CHAPTER 7

1. Rebecca Munnell McHugh et al., "Bridges and Barriers: Adolescent Perceptions of Student–Teacher Relationships," *Urban Education* 48, no. 1 (2013): 9–43.

2. Kent D. Peterson and Terrence E. Deal, "How Leaders Influence the Culture of Schools," *Educational Leadership* 56 (1998): 28.

3. Alexandra Loukas, Rie Suzuki, and Karissa D. Horton, "Examining School Connectedness as a Mediator of School Climate Effects," *Journal of Research on Adolescence* 16, no. 3 (2006): 491–502; Geoffrey D. Borman and N. Maritza Dowling, "Teacher Attrition and Retention: A Meta-Analytic and Narrative Review of the Research," *Review of Educational Research* 78, no. 3 (2008): 367–409; Jacquelynne S. Eccles and Robert W. Roeser, "Schools as Developmental Contexts During Adolescence," *Journal of Research on Adolescence* 21, no. 1 (2011): 225–241; Robert W. Roeser, Jacquelynne S. Eccles, and Arnold J. Sameroff, "School as a Context of Early Adolescents' Academic and Social-Emotional Development: A Summary of Research Findings," *Elementary School Journal* 100, no. 5 (2000): 443–471.

4. Ron Best, "Education, Support and the Development of the Whole Person," *British Journal of Guidance & Counselling* 36, no. 4 (2008): 343–351; Camille A. Farrington et al., "Teaching Adolescents to Become Learners: The Role of Noncognitive Factors in Shaping School Performance—A Critical Literature Review," University of Chicago Consortium on Chicago School Research, 2012; Anthony S. Bryk and Barbara Schneider, *Trust in Schools: A Core Resource for Improvement* (New York: Russell Sage Foundation, 2002); Megan

Tschannen-Moran, *Trust Matters: Leadership for Successful Schools* (New York: John Wiley & Sons, 2014).

5. Douglas C. Breunlin et al., "Personalizing a Large Comprehensive High School," *NASSP Bulletin* 89, no. 645 (2005): 24–42; Timothy J. Dyer, "Personalization: If Schools Don't Implement This One, There Will Be No Reform," *National Association of Secondary School Principals Bulletin* 80, no. 584 (1996): 1–8; Milbrey W. McLaughlin et al., "Constructing a Personalized School Environment," *Phi Delta Kappan* 72, no. 3 (1990): 230–235; Robert A. Cresswell and Patty Rasmussen, "Developing a Structure for Personalization in the High School," *National Association of Secondary School Principals Bulletin* 80, no. 584 (1996): 27–30.

6. Dyer, "Personalization: If Schools Don't Implement," 1–8.

7. McLaughlin et al., "Constructing a Personalized School Environment," 230, 231.

8. Stacey A. Rutledge et al., "Understanding Effective High Schools: Evidence for Personalization for Academic and Social Emotional Learning," *American Educational Research Journal* 52, no. 6 (2015): 1060–1092.

9. Kent D. Peterson and Terrence E. Deal, "How Leaders Influence the Culture of Schools," *Educational Leadership* 56 (1998): 28.

10. Dyer, "Personalization: If Schools Don't Implement."

11. Philip Hallinger and Ronald H. Heck, "Exploring the Principal's Contribution to School Effectiveness: 1980–1995," *School Effectiveness and School Improvement* 9, no. 2 (1998): 157–191; Angus J. MacNeil, Doris L. Prater, and Steve Busch, "The Effects of School Culture and Climate on Student Achievement," *International Journal of Leadership in Education* 12, no. 1 (2009): 73–84; Amrit Thapa et al., "A Review of School Climate Research," *Review of Educational Research* 83, no. 3 (2013): 357–385.

12. Breunlin et al., "Personalizing A Large Comprehensive High School," 24–42.

13. David W. Johnson, "Student–Student Interaction: The Neglected Variable in Education," *Educational Researcher* 10, no. 1 (1981): 5–10.

14. Nel Noddings, "An Ethic of Caring and Its Implications for Instructional Arrangements," *American Journal of Education* 96, no. 2 (1988): 215–230, especially 219; Maureen T. Hallinan, "Teacher Influences on Students' Attachment to School," *Sociology of Education* 81, no. 3 (2008): 271–283; John M. Jenkins and James W. Keefe, "A Special

Section on Personalized Instruction—Two Schools: Two Approaches to Personalized Learning," *Phi Delta Kappan* 83, no. 6 (2002): 449–456.

15. Johnson, "Student–Student Interaction."

16. Joseph A. Durlak et al., "The Impact of Enhancing Students' Social and Emotional Learning: A Meta-Analysis of School-Based Universal Interventions," *Child Development* 82, no. 1 (January 1, 2011): 405–32; Roger Weissberg and Jason Cascarino, "Academic Learning+ Social-Emotional Learning= National Priority," *Phi Delta Kappan* 95, no. 2 (2013): 8–13.

17. Leslie Santee Siskin, and Judith Warren Little, "The Subject Department: Continuities and Critiques," in *The Subjects in Question: Departmental Organization and the High School*, ed. Leslie Santee Siskin and Judith Warren Little (New York: Teachers College Press, 1995), 32–49; Susan S. Stodolsky and Pamela L. Grossman, "The Impact of Subject Matter on Curricular Activity: An Analysis of Five Academic Subjects," *American Educational Research Journal*, 32, no. 2 (1995): 227–249.

18. Andrew Guest and Barbara Schneider, "Adolescents' Extracurricular Participation in Context: The Mediating Effects of Schools, Communities, and Identity," *Sociology of Education* (2003): 89–109.

19. Stephen C. Peck et al., "Exploring the Roles of Extracurricular Activity Quantity and Quality in the Educational Resilience of Vulnerable Adolescents: Variable- and Pattern-Centered Approaches," *Journal of Social Issues* 64, no. 1 (2008): 135–156.; Benjamin G. Gibbs et al., "Extracurricular Associations and College Enrollment," *Social Science Research* 50 (2015): 367–381.

20. Guest and Schneider, "Adolescents' Extracurricular Participation."

21. Karen A. Randolph and Jeannette L. Johnson, "School-Based Mentoring Programs: A Review of the Research," *Children & Schools* 30, no. 3 (2008): 177–185.

22. Christina M. Underhill, "The Effectiveness of Mentoring Programs in Corporate Settings: A Meta-Analytical Review of the Literature," *Journal of Vocational Behavior* 68, no. 2 (2006): 292–307.

23. Michael Karcher, "Increases in Academic Connectedness and Self-Esteem Among High School Students Who Serve as Cross-Age Peer Mentors," *Professional School Counseling* 12, no. 4 (2009): 2156759X0901200403.

24. Anthony S. Bryk et al., *Organizing Schools for Improvement: Lessons from Chicago* (Chicago: University of Chicago Press, 2010); Chris

Dolejs, "Report on Key Practices and Policies of Consistently Higher Performing High Schools," National High School Center, 2006; Ellen Goldring et al., "Assessing Learning-Centered Leadership: Connections to Research, Professional Standards, and Current Practices," *Leadership and Policy in Schools* 8, no. 1 (2009): 1–36; Valerie E. Lee, Anthony S. Bryk, and Julia B. Smith, "Chapter 5: The Organization of Effective Secondary Schools," *Review of Research in Education* 19, no. 1 (1993): 171–267.

CHAPTER 8

1. Diane Ravitch, *The Great School Wars: A History of the New York City Public Schools* (Baltimore: Johns Hopkins University Press, 2000); David B. Tyack, *The One Best System: A History of American Urban Education* (Cambridge, MA: Harvard University Press, 1974).
2. David B. Tyack and Larry Cuban, *Tinkering Toward Utopia: A Century of Public School Reform* (Cambridge, MA: Harvard University Press, 1995).
3. Elena Silva Taylor White and Thomas Toch, "The Carnegie Unit: A Century-Old Standard in a Changing Education Landscape," Carnegie Foundation for the Advancement of Teaching, 2015.
4. Claudia Goldin, "America's Graduation from High School: The Evolution and Spread of Secondary Schooling in the Twentieth Century," *Journal of Economic History* 58, no. 2 (1998): 345–374; National Center for Education Statistics, "Public High School Graduation Rates," last updated May 2019, https://nces.ed.gov/programs/coe/indicator_coi.asp.
5. ACT, Inc., *The Condition of College & Career Readiness 2016: National* (Iowa City, IA: ACT, 2016); Peter L. Benson, *All Kids Are Our Kids* (San Francisco: Jossey-Bass, 2006).
6. Tyack and Cuban, *Tinkering Toward Utopia*, 51.
7. Robert L. Hampel, *The Last Little Citadel: American High Schools Since 1940* (Boston: Houghton Mifflin, 1986).
8. Tyack and Cuban, 1995, 52.
9. Diane Ravitch, *National Standards in American Education* (Washington, DC: Brookings Institution, 1995); Neil J. Smelser and Sydney Halpern, "The Historical Triangulation of Family, Economy, and Education," *American Journal of Sociology* 84 (1978): S288–S315.
10. Hampel, *The Last Citadel*.
11. Doris Rhea Coy, "The Role and Training of the School Counselor: Background and Purpose," *National Association of Secondary School Principals Bulletin* 83, no. 603 (1999): 2–8.

12. National Commission on Excellence in Education. "A Nation at Risk: The Imperative for Educational Reform," *Elementary School Journal* 84, no. 2 (1983): 113–130, especially 116.
13. Christopher Mazzeo et al., "Improving High School Success: Searching for Evidence of Promise," *Teachers College Record* 118, no. 13 (2016): 13.
14. Theodore R. Sizer, *Horace's Compromise: The Dilemma of the American High School* (New York: Houghton Mifflin Harcourt, 2004), 6.
15. Coalition of Essential Schools, "Common Principles," accessed September 26, 2019, http://essentialschools.org/common-principles.
16. Coalition of Essential Schools, "Continuous School Improvement," accessed September 26, 2019, http://essentialschools.org/continuous-school-improvement.
17. Thomas Hatch, "What Does It Take to 'Go to Scale'? Reflections on the Promise and the Perils of Comprehensive School Reform," *Journal of Education for Students Placed at Risk* 5, no. 4 (2000): 339–354.
18. Francesca A. Lopez, "Altering the Trajectory of the Self-Fulfilling Prophecy: Asset-Based Pedagogy and Classroom Dynamics," *Journal of Teacher Education* 68, no. 2 (2017): 193–212.
19. Khara L. Pence, Laura M. Justice, and Alice K. Wiggins, "Preschool Teachers' Fidelity in Implementing a Comprehensive Language-Rich Curriculum," *Language, Speech, and Hearing Services in Schools* 39 (July 2008): 329–341.
20. Mark Berends, Susan Bodilly, and Sheila Nataraj Kirby, *Facing the Challenges of Whole-School Reform: New American Schools after a Decade*, MR-1498-EDU (Santa Monica, CA: Rand, 2002), www.rand.org/pubs/research_briefs/RB8019/index1.html; Thomas K. Glennan et al., *Expanding the Reach of Education Reforms: Perspectives from Leaders in the Scale-Up of Educational Interventions* (Santa Monica, CA: Rand, 2000).
21. Lora Cohen-Vogel et al., "A Model of Continuous Improvement in High Schools: A Process for Research, Innovation Design, Implementation, and Scale," *Teachers College Record* 116, no. 13 (2016): 1–26.
22. Barry J. Fishman et al., *Design-Based Implementation Research: Theories, Methods, and Exemplars* (New York: National Society for the Study of Education, 2013); Anthony S. Bryk et al., *Learning to Improve: How America's Schools Can Get Better at Getting Better* (Cambridge, MA: Harvard Education Press, 2015).
23. Chris Dede, "Scaling Up: Evolving Innovations Beyond Ideal Settings to Challenging Contexts of Practice," in *Cambridge Handbook of the*

Learning Sciences, ed. R. Keith Sawyer (Cambridge, UK: Cambridge University Press, 2006), 551–566.

24. Cynthia E. Coburn, "Rethinking Scale: Moving Beyond Numbers to Deep and Lasting Change," *Educational Researcher* 32, no. 6 (August 1, 2003): 3–12, https://doi.org/10.3102/0013189X032006003.

25. Chris Redding, Marisa Cannata, and Katherine Taylor Haynes, "With Scale in Mind: NCSU's Integrated Model of School-Based Design and Implementation," *Peabody Journal of Education* 92, no. 5 (2017): 589–608.

26. Coburn, "Rethinking Scale."

27. World Bank, "Scaling-Up the Impact of Good Practices in Rural Development: A Working Paper to Support Implementation of the World Bank's Rural Development Strategy" (Washington, D.C.: The International Bank for Reconstruction and Development, Agriculture and Rural Development Department, 2003), www-wds.worldbank.org/external/default/WDSContentServer/WDSP/IB/2004/01/30/000160016_20040130163125/Rendered/PDF/260310White0co1e1up1final1formatted.pdf.

Acknowledgments

Our research practice partnership with Broward County Public Schools in Florida has spanned nine years, multiple universities, and three external partners. Funded by two large grants from the U.S. Department of Education, our research benefited from the time and effort across institutions and organizations that were required to identify Personalization for Academic and Social-Emotional Learning (PASL), develop it into a viable reform, support its implementation, and study its effectiveness.

The National Center on Scaling Up Effective Schools (NCSU), funded by an Institute of Education Sciences (IES) Research and Development Center program (R305C10023), was established in 2010 as a partnership between Broward County Public Schools, Fort Worth Independent School District in Texas, Vanderbilt University, Florida State University, University of Wisconsin at Madison, and the Education Development Center (EDC). The EDC provided critical design and professional-development support. As the years progressed, the University of North Carolina at Chapel Hill and Georgia State University joined as partners. In 2016, after the IES grant ended, we received new funding from the Investing in Innovation (i3) program (U411C160107) to continue the work and externally evaluate PASL. For this grant, Broward County

Public Schools, Florida State University, and Vanderbilt University joined as partners with Norman Merrifield from 808Education, our professional-development provider, and RTI International, our external evaluator.

Across these multiple institutions, we wish to acknowledge many people. Lora Cohen-Vogel from the University of North Carolina at Chapel Hill and Tom Smith at the University of California at Riverside worked with Marisa to write the original NCSU grant. During these first years with Lora and Tom, we were joined weekly by Ellen Goldring, Joseph Murphy, and Katherine Taylor Haynes at Vanderbilt as we established the path forward. La'Tara Osborne-Lampkin, Jason Huff, and Courtney Preston also participated in the project in the early years. We worked closely with the EDC team—Dr. Cheryl King, Tom Haferd, Anne Wang, Eliza Fabillar, Frank DeVito, Maria-Paz Avery, and Cindy Mata-Aguilar as they brought us through the design-team process and two years of continuous improvement cycles at quarterly meetings and the annual Summer Institutes. Gabrielle Chapman, Christine Neumerski, Georgine Pion, Mollie Rubin, and Sandra Wilson at Vanderbilt joined later to help continue the momentum. We were also joined by Patrice Iatarola at Florida State and Tim Sass at Georgia State University; Tim conducted our first evaluation. We thank Jeff Rosen and his team at RTI for conducting the external evaluation required by the i3 grant.

The NCSU Advisory Board provided valuable insight at critical moments early on in the process. We extend our appreciation to Alfredo Artiles, Cynthia Coburn, Ron Ferguson, Louis Gomez, Carolyn Herrington, Tom Payzant, Don Peurach, Russell Rumberger, and Barbara Schneider.

The grants funded numerous graduate students, many of whom have graduated and now work in academic and nonprofit organizations. At Florida State University, we thank Jennifer Blalock,

Lynn Comer, Saralyn Grass, Kitchka Petrova, Ronnie Roberts, and Bruce Vinyard. At the University of North Carolina at Chapel Hill, we thank Christopher Harrison, Danielle Allen, Allison Rose-Sokol, Ariel Tichnor-Wagner, John Wachen, and Qi Xing. At Vanderbilt University, we thank Samantha Adler, Mary Batiwalla, Laura Booker, Tim Drake, Chaundra Gipson, James Guthrie, Chelsea Henkel, Seth Hunter, Ela Joshi, Emily Kern, Chunyun Li, Jason Miller, Erin Milligan-Mattes, Tuan Nguyen, Susan Kemper Patrick, Russ Ramsey, Christopher Redding, Jenna Rush, Victoria Sears, and Daniella Torre. Two graduate students, Stephanie and Ronnie Roberts, also used NCSU data for their dissertations. Brittany Closson-Pitts and Elizabeth Gilliam at Florida State and Mary Frances Street at Vanderbilt continue to work on the i3 grant. We also thank them and Veronica Chase, another i3 graduate assistant, for their support and feedback on the early drafts of this book. Vanderbilt staff members Tammy Eidson, Carolyn Fatheree, Tenesa Davis, Pat Abelson, and Lyn Strevell provided important administrative support. At FSU, we thank Jennifer Ramsey, Stacy Fletcher, Terra Bradley, and Russ Walker in the College of Education's Office of Research.

PASL has also been supported by private donations through matching funds of the i3 grant. For their generous support to the professional development activities in Broward, we thank the Community Foundation of Broward, the Helios Foundation, the Phoenix Fund, Cynthia Schumacher, Nina Shuman, and Ellen and Rod Thornton. We also extend our gratitude to the Alumni and Friends of the Florida State University College of Education.

At Florida State University, we also thank College of Education deans Marcy Driscoll, Damon Andrews, and Bob Reiser; and the Florida State University Foundation members Kevin Derryberry, David Lipen, and Larissa Trygg, all of whom worked to raise these funds and support these grants.

Our deepest thanks go to Broward County Public Schools educators, who through their enthusiasm and thoughtful participation engaged from the very beginning with the idea that they could improve their schools by understanding what higher performing schools did well and turn that into something systemic that could be applied in other schools both in their county and beyond. We thank the original Design Team members, some of whom are featured in this book— Armando Abreu, Norman Alford, Lori Canning, Matt Dearen, Brad Fatout, Derek Gordon, Lisa Herron, Cherie Hodgson-Toeller, Harriet Ivey, Brian King, Kristie Knapp, Wendolyn Mola, Jill Samaroo, and Peter Tiernan. We also thank the School Design Team members of the original pilot schools who played a critical role in transforming PASL from a reform with five components into a living entity that now shapes adult-student relationships and processes in Broward County Public Schools: Cinderella Ashley-Hill, Dedrian Beason, Andrew Bennett, Charlene Brown, Natalie Carter, Christine Cerbon, June Cole, Simon Dritz, Ann-Marie Ewart-Gilbert, Rafeal Frim, Javier Gonzales, Robert Goodwin, Carla Knight, Kienna Knowles, Jo Lantowski, Virginia Maskell, Stephane Monereau, Sara Neugaard, Christina Pellicer, Kristin Potter, Donna Robinson, Judy Segesta, Hubert Simon, Malcolm Spence, Vivian Suarez, John Tienjaroonkui, Kathleen Weathers, Jodie Weinstein, Antonio Williams, and Kimberly Williams. We also thank the numerous principals, particularly of the original eight schools, including Jimmy Arrojo, Scott Fiske, Angel Gomez, Theresa Hall, Dr. Karlton Johnson, Michelle Kefford, James Neer, and Hudson Thomas, as well as the other participating principals and assistant principals across the years, especially Derek Gordon, Luis Espinosa, Mark Hoffman, Dr. Tameka King, Dr. Susan Robinson, and Carla Hozebin.

Hundreds of teachers have participated in PASL over the five years of implementation, both at quarterly meetings and at their schools. Because of their involvement and feedback, the reform has grown and matured. Thousands of Broward County Public Schools students have gone through high school since the grant began. Through their participation in PASL and in our research project, they described for us their experiences in high school as well as their experiences as PASL students. Gaining their perspectives and hearing their voices has been critical to our understanding of the importance of a present and caring adult in their lives.

This partnership would not have flourished without the district leaders who embraced the vision of PASL and provided leadership and support. These include Superintendent Robert Runcie, Dr. Valerie Wanza, Ralph Aiello, Jeff Stanley, and past district leaders Dr. Leontine Butler and Dr. Desmond Blackburn. We also thank Alan Strauss and Michael Ramirez, the Cadre Directors who led PASL at the district level for five years, fully believing in its power to transform schools and provide more opportunities for students.

We would also like to extend our gratitude to Caroline Chauncey, our editor at Harvard Education Press, for her vision, persistence, and invaluable feedback. May everyone be as fortunate to have an editor like her.

We must also acknowledge the support of our families, as we spent much time away in Broward County at network meetings or doing fieldwork. Over these past nine years, we have had children and grandchildren enter our families and begin to leave the nest.

In February 2018, Broward County Public Schools experienced a terrible tragedy and collective trauma when a mass shooter killed seventeen students and teachers and injured seventeen more at Marjory Stoneman Douglas High School. We grieved with them and recognized the challenges the district and school educators and students faced in the aftermath.

Personalization in schools sounds like a simple idea. We were told many times by educators in Broward County that it was something that good schools and good teachers do already. Yet personalization is clearly difficult to enact in practice, as educators and students negotiate multiple pressures and demands. We believe that the participation of everyone mentioned here helped bring this idea to scale throughout Broward County Public Schools and improved student experiences in those schools.

The research for this book was conducted with funding from the Institute of Education Sciences (R305C10023). The opinions expressed in this book are those of the authors and do not necessarily represent the views of the sponsor.

The contents of this book were developed under a grant from the US Department of Education, Investing in Innovation (i3) Program. However, those contents do not necessarily represent the policy of the US Department of Education, and readers should not assume endorsement by the federal government.

About the Authors

Stacey A. Rutledge is Associate Professor in the Department of Educational Leadership and Policy Studies at the Florida State University. She is currently serving as the Florida State University investigator in the National Center on Scaling Up Effective Schools, a center funded by the US Department of Education and aimed at identifying the policies and practices of effective high schools. Her research explores how policies and approaches aimed at improving teaching and learning, such as test-based accountability, continuous improvement, and data use, shape the work of district and school administrators and teachers and, ultimately, students' learning opportunities. She also studies the use of social media by students and educators in secondary schools. She has published articles in various journals, including the *American Educational Research Journal*, the *American Journal of Education*, and the *Teachers College Record*. She is a coeditor of *The Infrastructure of Accountability: Data Use and the Transformation of American Education*, published by Harvard Education Press, and coauthor of *The Education Mayor: How Mayors Improve School Performance*. She has also been a high school social studies and English teacher.

Marisa Cannata is a Research Associate Professor in the Peabody College of Education and Human Development at Vanderbilt

University. As Director of the National Center on Scaling Up Effective Schools, Dr. Cannata has overseen its district partnerships and has worked collaboratively with Broward County Public Schools to scale and sustain the PASL innovation. Dr. Cannata's substantive expertise focuses on continuous-improvement research and scaling up, charter schools, teacher career decisions and evaluation, teacher leadership, and teacher experiences with reform. She is the coeditor of *School Choice and School Improvement*, published by Harvard Education Press, and *Mapping the High School Reform Landscape*, a yearbook by Teachers College Record. Dr. Cannata has a PhD in educational policy from Michigan State University and has published in the *Journal of Educational Administration*, the *Educational Researcher*, *Education Finance and Policy*, the *Educational Administration Quarterly*, the *Journal of Educational Change*, and the *Elementary School Journal*.

Stephanie L. Brown is an Assistant Professor at York College of Pennsylvania in the Department of Education. She currently teaches courses on assessment and the instructional needs of English language learners to preservice teachers. Dr. Brown's research interests are rooted in her diverse experience as an elementary teacher in Broward County Public Schools and Seminole County Public Schools, a teacher of English for Speakers of Other Languages (ESOL) in China, and a professional-development facilitator in Nigeria. These interests include qualitative investigations of research practice partnerships in education, intermediary organizations, and teacher policy and reform. Before joining York College, Stephanie worked with the National Center on Scaling Up Effective Schools (NCSU) and the National Center for Research in Policy and Practice. Dr. Brown has a PhD in foundations of education from Florida State University, with an emphasis on international and comparative education. Her dissertation focused on the relational dynamics of the NCSU partnership in its design phase. She has published articles in the *Teachers College Record* and the *Peabody Journal of Education* and has presented her work at multiple national and regional conferences.

Daniel G. Traeger has been working with the National Center for Scaling Up Effective Schools as District Liaison Representative with Florida Broward County Public Schools since 2012. He has served as a high school principal for thirteen years, as well as an assistant principal and a middle school principal. He also coordinated and supervised the implementation of Broward County's districtwide secondary school redesign, working with thirty high schools serving diverse student populations, and he was appointed designee for the district's Small Learning Community Grant. He was chosen as Principal of the Year in 2010 by the Florida Parent Teacher Association and in 2011 by the Florida Association of Student Councils. His two high schools, West Broward and Marjory Stoneman Douglas, were designated premier high schools in the nation by the College Board. Out of seven thousand high schools, West Broward High School was recognized for closing achievement gaps for Hispanics and African Americans; the school ranked fourteenth in the nation for Hispanic students and eightieth in the nation for African American students enrolled in Advanced Placement courses.

Index